THE HOUSE GUESTS

An Account of Life with Two Cats,
Including Some Random Comment
on Other Matters, as Well as Stories
of Incidental Beasts, among Them
One Goose.

The
HOUSE GUESTS

John D. MacDonald

Illustrated with photographs

A FAWCETT GOLD MEDAL BOOK

Fawcett Publications, Inc., Greenwich, Connecticut

The
HOUSE GUESTS

FOREWORD

This is not a luvums-duvums-itsyboo book, about pooty-tats.

I keep forgetting who said what, and am generally too impatient to trace it down. Someone said: Sentimentality is unearned emotion.

It would be a strange injustice to the breed to write a sentimental book about Roger and Geoffrey. House cats are implacable realists. Their affections are as honest as their lust for the hunt. Their vanity is not diluted by any lack of confidence. Their codes of behavior are based upon an essential dignity which, in careful proportion, demands and awards respect.

Portions of this book may strike the pretty-kitty set as being unnecessarily unpleasant. Without apology I say that life for any mammal from mouse to man is a precarious and bloody gamble wherein, despite the most astute management of resources and shrewdness of play, the house percentage will eventually win.

I am beginning this account in the spring of 1964. Roger the Lodger, sometimes known as Gladys, is downstairs drowsing on the corner of the sill of the picture window overlooking a blue mile of Little Sarasota Bay. Should he survive until September of this year, he will be nineteen years old. His half brother, Geoffrey, died during the summer of 1960, a few months past his fourteenth birthday.

Dorothy and I, in talking over the episodes and impressions which make up this book, are aware of our tendency to anthropomorphize these house-guest beasts, to attribute to them awareness and responses beyond their capacities. In so doing, we have perhaps made too generous interpretations of observed behavior. Such generosity is inevitably a product of affection. As is so true of children, the cherished cat is inevitably exceptional.

Though it is considered bad artistic judgment to state bluntly the theme of any book, and quite possibly pretentious to infer that a pet book can have such a weighty increment, I herewith state my pot of message: When any higher order of animal is given security, attention, affection, and treated in a consistent and predictable manner, that animal will respond with a continuing revelation of those factors of intelligence and personality which differentiate it from the norm of the breed. This is especially true of both cats and people. The barn cat, in the hard bargain of shelter in return for mousing, withdraws to that standardized catness which the uninitiated think typical of all cats regardless of vocation. Were a Martian to observe us only in throngs, during our surly passages to and from work, he might think us a sorry and unrewarding species indeed and generalize about us in an unflattering way.

Though the house cats will respond to a trusted environment in astonishing ways, their reactions will be related to varying quotients of intelligence and personality, even as you and I. If Roger seems to take over more than his share of the episodic account, it is not because he was the first acquired and has survived longest, nor is it because his intelligence is greater than was Geoffrey's, but rather because his personality—clown, neurotic, reckless hero, inept hunter, nag, hypochondriac, experimenter—shows more deviation from the anticipated norm than did Geoffrey's.

Another aspect is worth comment. With half of the world's billions on such short rations that a few hundred calories can make the difference between survival and disaster, there is an effete and trivial overtone to the pet-keeping habit. Yet I cannot help but sense herein some supra-historical instinct more constant than the contemporary economics of starvation. We and our domesticated animals have shared hundreds of thousands of years of a precarious mutual existence on this whirling mudball, have tested the scents borne on ancient winds, died in the same rude tempests, bled the same color, feared the same darkness, protected our young with the same desperate instinct. We have shared this journey, and now in a world where we are busily interposing more layers of plastic, paper, transistors, and asphalt between ourselves and reality, where we are poisoning the air, the earth, and the waters in our hot wars against insects and our cold wars against each other, it is a needful reminder to have, close at hand, that striped, furry camouflage, that functional honesty of fang and talon, the sleekness of the muscles of the hunt. In its best form the relationship is ceremonial-symbiotic, composed of grave courtesies and considerations, a sharing rather than an ownership structure. In its worst form, wherein the dignity of both species is degraded, it is suffocatingly pooty-tat.

I can not properly dedicate this book to the two cats. In 1960 Simon and Schuster published a suspense novel of mine entitled *The End of the Night*. As a result of a momentary attack of the quaints, the dedication reads, "To Roger and Geoffrey, who left their marks on the manuscript."

In an abashed penance, I dedicate this book to all those doctors of veterinary medicine who, despite all the cutenesses of the pooty-tat trade, have retained a respect, liking, and consideration for animals on their own primitive terms. In these affluent days of the teeny cashmere sweaters, tiny electric blankets, pedicures, exotic diets, and dear little kitty-coffins, such gentlemen are becoming ever

9

more rare. The ones mentioned in this account are included in this dedication.

Sarasota, Florida
April 2, 1964

ONE

I grew up with a smooth-haired fox terrier named Prince. He was acquired before I started school and was still living when I went off to college. When I was little, he was very much the country dog. We lived in Sharon, Pennsylvania. We had a summer cottage on the Pymatuning River in Orangeville, Ohio.

Much to my mother's indignation and despair, Prince buddied up with a jovial pack of farm dogs and would run off with them on a periodic debauch, which involved hurrying down to a country slaughterhouse and rolling in some pungent horror, and coming home wearing a bashful and guilty smirk. The invariable procedure was to put on gloves, take him out along the boathouse dock, and eject him into the river. After this was repeated three or four times, the stench was diminished to the point where he could be washed. He came to expect this as the inevitable end result of fragrant holiday and as a price which, though he made a great show of reluctance, he was willing to pay.

It was a canine variation of a night in the drunk tank. When he was at last clean, his morale was excellent.

My maternal grandfather was an avid hunter of the Ohio woodchuck, and Prince became of such value in this patient sport my grandfather bragged about him to anyone who would listen.

When my father went with another company, we moved to Utica, New York, and Prince made the transition from country dog to city dog. We lived on Beverly Place in Utica, and across the street lived a rugged Airedale named Mike. He belonged to the Robinson Family. My kid sister, Doris, later married Bill Robinson. It became Mike's mission to kill the overconfident fox terrier across the street. Their brawls were loud, bloody, and in deadly earnest. Prince was outclassed. We managed to separate them in time, every time.

My grandfather developed an effective system. There was an old turret-top refrigerator in the back hallway at that time. He kept a supply of very loud flash crackers and kitchen matches atop the refrigerator. At the first sounds of combat he would run out, light a firecracker, and toss it into the snarling turmoil. The bang would send both dogs screaming in opposite directions. In time truce was established, and thereafter they ignored each other, with the infrequent exception of a mild sneer at long range.

With his learning process accelerated by being bowled over without serious injury by a passing car, Prince took over that porky-wise manner of the city dog, the broad-chested little trot, the obvious preoccupation with destination, interrupted by the routine examinations of light poles and tree trunks.

A friend phoned us once and told us of Prince's solution to the traffic-light problem. We followed him and saw how he managed it. At the foot of the Beverly Place hill, a block away, Beverly Place crossed Genesee Street, US Route 5, a four-lane street, heavily traveled, with a traffic light at the corner. Prince would stop at the corner and begin to bark. Sharp, peremptory barks, widely spaced. The light would turn. Traffic would stop. He would thereupon trot across the wide street staying within the pedestrian stripes, quite obviously convinced that he had demanded a favor and that, as always, it had been granted.

I am convinced that after I went off to the University of Pennsylvania my subsequent relationship with Prince was a disappointment to my parents. After all, this was A Boy and His Dog, reunited during school vacations. But I had to force more enthusiasm than I felt, and his response also seemed somewhat stylized. I used to wonder if I was lacking in capacity for this sort of affection. I realize now that the world had broadened for both of us. We had gone separate ways and had other things on our minds. I was learning to bark at another kind of traffic light. Our relationship was mildly affable and slightly nostalgic.

When I met my wife-to-be at Syracuse University in 1936, Dorothy owned a cowardly black cocker spaniel whose registered name was Shadowfall Chloe. Chloe was utterly convinced of imminent disaster from almost any direction. On leash, when the horrors got too much for her, she would scrunch onto her belly and have to be either picked up and carried or dragged along with an ugly grating of toenails. If I reached slowly to pat her during our early acquaintanceship, she would run, screaming, and hide in the most remote corner she could find. Her eyes rolled white amid that black hair and she would pant with terror. Asleep she whined constantly, legs twitching as she fled the demons.

After Dorothy and I were married, Chloe gave me a dubious acceptance.

In our innocence of the wiles of dogdom, we had her bred at a kennel other than the one of her origin, with a pick-of-the-litter arrangement for the sire. When her time came, we took her to the kennel and left her there for the birthing. When we returned an attendant showed us one very tiny dead blond cocker in a tin can and said that she had given birth to just one, and that was it. Sorry. It was dead because she had gotten out somehow and had it in the cold. Sorry.

We now know that a litter of one is so improbable as to be a fair indication of hankypanky. Perhaps Chloe's conviction the world is a deadly place was justified. After all, they did steal her children.

In 1938 Dorothy and I and Chloe were living in a fourth-floor walk-up apartment in Cambridge, Massachusetts, in what had once been a Harvard dormitory. Its doubtless apocryphal claim to notoriety was that during its dormitory days one Lucius Beebe, with the assistance of some interested companions, had dropped a piano down the stair well onto the tiled ground-level floor to see what the impact would sound like.

I was attending the Harvard Graduate School of Business Administration. Dorothy was pregnant with our only child, now twenty-five. She was working for the Kelling Nut Company with an assigned route which included an eerie number of urban and suburban drugstores. We were trying to either break our lease or get permission to sublet from the brothers who then owned the building. The obstetrician had advised us strongly to move out of a fourth-floor walk-up. In presenting this problem to one of the brothers at his office I had been somewhat disheartened to have him say to me, "Listen, you, if you're both dead we collect from your estate. You gotta lease."

It was a weekday evening. Dorothy was napping. I was working on a case assignment for a class. Dorothy woke up and said, "John, this building is shaking. It must be a hurricane."

It was a chunky brick building. This was obviously some imaginative nonsense associated with pregnancy. They never have hurricanes in New England. I told her it was nonsense. She told me to turn the radio on.

The radio said, ". . . and martial law has just been declared in Worcester. Winds are now upward of eighty miles an hour and the storm center moves . . ."

We had a little black tudor Ford sedan parked down in front, and as it was not permitted to leave it there all night, I always took it over and put it in the lot across the river behind the Business School and usually combined this errand with the one of walking Chloe. So I snapped Chloe's leash onto her harness ring and left at once. The winds seemed very strong, but not alarmingly so until I got onto the Charles River Bridge. Then I was broadsided with such violence I nearly lost control.

I put the car behind the Business School. I got out. As soon as I got a few feet away from the car, the wind got a good purchase on me, and before I could brace myself or grab anything, I was off and running, clutching the leash, Chloe bounding and sliding and screeching along with me. I came up against the woven-wire backstop of the tennis courts. Over the impressive and constant scream of the wind I heard an ungodly banshee howl that went rowwa-rowwer-rooee and soon identified it as a sound made by huge sheets of metal being ripped off the roof of one of the Business School buildings and flying by, spinning in flight, about fifty feet over my head. I think that it was at this moment Chloe's defeat became total. All her life she had known of pending horror.

I could not pick her up. I needed both hands to hold onto things. Later we learned that was the absolute peak of wind velocity, unmeasured because everything it could have been measured by was blown away. The velocity was measured by the damage done in that hour I was gone from the apartment. With the loop of the dog's leash over my right wrist, I struggled homeward, crouching and crawling, seeking shelter, zigzagging from one precarious hand hold to the next. When we got to the bridge the wind was picking up solid water and dumping it on the bridge. It ran ankle-deep at both ends. I stayed below the shelter of the rail. I had to drag that damned dog. She was flattened, legs tucked under, eyes shut. When I reached the corner at the Harvard College side, every last one of those huge elms had come down since I had driven under them not long before. They lay blocking the road, three and four feet in diameter, with big slabs of sidewalk uptilted by the towering root structure. They did provide a wind-break. I had to lift Chloe over three of them. When we got to the sidewalk the wind was behind me. Chloe was rigid, inert.

About fifty yards from the apartment building, she had a chance to express that final edge of terror. Dragging her along, I heard a curious clanging behind us, coming closer, over the wind sound. I looked back and saw an empty garbage can coming end over end, right up the sidewalk. It was hitting about every twenty feet, and at the apex of each leap it was perhaps four feet off the sidewalk. As I dodged and gave Chloe a yank to pull her out of the way, she turned and looked at the horrible thing clanging down upon her. I have never heard a scream like that from a dog. She sounded like a veteran Hitchcock actress. Galvanized, she ran to the end of the leash with such spirit that when she came to the end of it, it snapped her over onto her back. She lay right there, paws curled, belly exposed, waiting for the huge, noisy thing to come eat her. It clanged on by.

After I got her home, after she had been dried and brushed, she still shook. She tried some of that strange little talking sound dogs attempt at times. But she gave it up. She just did not have the vocabulary for it. After that, curiously enough, her timidity was not as evident. But I cannot believe it was valor. It seemed more like resignation, as though she had decided that flight itself was futile. Later, when we had to move to a dogless environment, we gave her to friends in Poland, New York. I cannot believe they found her very responsive. No one did. But it *was* fun calling her.

I spent two and a half years overseas. Dorothy and Johnny moved into an upstairs apartment in a two-story frame house in Utica, New York, at 1109 State Street. She wrote me about the acquisition of a dog. They had heard of a litter of pups at the pound which sounded interesting, and they went to look at them, but they both became captivated by a whiskery little female with a most persuasive personality, who, from the pictures I have seen, apparently had some Skye terrier in her bloodline. They took her home and named her Toppy.

From all reports, she was a splendid dog, extremely bright, affectionate, responsive. She soon learned the pleasant duty of going and fetching her leash when told she was about to go for a walk.

Dorothy found land for a victory garden atop Deerfield Hill overlooking North Utica and a broad reach of the placid valley of the Mohawk. It belonged to a farmer who lived a little further north along Route 8. In that spring of 1944 they went up there often, the woman, the child, and the lively dog. The farmer plowed the land for them, and Dorothy raised great hampers of vegetables.

One day they started back toward the car and, as they reached the road, Toppy ran on ahead. Traffic was light, gas was rationed, and the speed limit in all of New York State was forty miles an hour. A woman alone in a car heading north struck and killed the dog. She saw the dog. She made a halfhearted attempt to avoid it, knew she struck it, and kept on going.

(Lady, if you have survived these twenty years, do you still remember? Do you remember the summer day, the blond, tall girl and the little blond boy and the panic in their voices as they called their lively little dog? You may not remember them, but believe me, they will never forget you—nor forgive you the ugliness of not bothering to stop.)

Awash with tears they went to the farmer and borrowed a spade and buried the dog under a tree near where she had been killed. We go up that road often, because we take Route 8 to go from Utica to Piseco Lake where we have a summer cottage. During a hundred trips either Dorothy or Johnny would say, "There's Toppy's tree."

The tree is gone now. A year or so ago the State Highway Department "improved" Route 8 between Utica and Poland. They did not widen the road itself. They widened the shoulders and bulldozed away those few thousand trees which gave that drive beauty and a character all its own. Now it looks like any other road through pleasant, rolling country.

It is unfortunate for all of the rest of us that the trade of highway engineering should inevitably attract just the kind of dreary, narrow, empty little fellow whose only feeling about a tree is a vague uneasiness that someday someone might drive forty feet off the road and run into it. He prefers to clear away all such unplanned nastiness and leave us an unimpeded view of huge paper people showing their gigantic tombstone teeth as they smoke, drink, nibble, drive, and rub on consumer products which apparently

17

create for them unimaginable ecstasies and social conquests.

I do not know the sterling trade qualifications of the man who planned the present sterility of Route 8 between Poland and Utica, but aesthetically he is a fink. He took Toppy's tree—and several thousand others which offended his sense of ugliness. It is astonishing how many hundred years of charm can be negated in one afternoon by some power-smitten snert at a drawing board.

My mother tried to fill the teary gap by giving Johnny a little pedigree blanket cocker pup. It was too far gone with worms to survive the harsh remedy. But another dog did seem a good idea, and Dorothy acquired a young male cocker spaniel, black, which Johnny named Jive.

After I was liberated at Dix, we holidayed in New York and then, in that September of 1945, headed up the prethruway highways toward Utica. Dorothy in a very tentative manner told me about the Problem with Jive. At first she made him sound merely unreliable. He seemed quite willing to bite people. She had to tie him outside stores. She had taken out special insurance, just in case.

The dog had been playing with Johnny and had suddenly snarled and bitten him on the lip. Johnny had required medical attention. The dog had been eating a bone under the kitchen table. Dorothy had walked by. As she did so he had snarled, snapped, and somehow yanked the whole foot of her stocking out through the open toe of her sandal.

The people who had bred him had taken him back for a little while for retraining, and he had seemed better, and then he had gotten worse. By then I was quite willing to agree with her tentative diagnosis. Jive was nuts. Not just unpredictably, but dangerously demented.

She suggested I go to the kennel and get him by myself and bring him home so I would have an objective chance to observe him. She would leave it up to me as to whether I thought he should be destroyed. He was at Dr. Sellman's kennel on North Genesee Street. The day after we got home, I went and got Jive. It was my first meeting with

Dr. Sellman. Staying within the bounds of ethical comment, he told me a few things about the dog's heritage. The breeding kennel had been having trouble with bad-tempered cockers, and in this instance there seemed to be considerable malevolence on the part of both the sire and the bitch. Also, their quaint training program seemed to consist of flailing away at the naughty dog with a stick, "to show him who was boss."

He said the dog could probably be sold, and many people would think that a logical answer. But if I decided the dog was too dangerous to live with, a better ethical posture would be to have it destroyed. Better for the breed too. He would do it.

Jive seemed intent on proving I had nothing to worry about. He was a little wary of me, but no more than one would expect from any dog. He knew the car, and he quickly became quite friendly.

I stopped in town at the Ford garage to have some wiring checked under the dash. I took Jive out of the car and around to the rear bumper and tied his leash to it, so he could not take a taste of the mechanic working on the wiring.

I roamed restlessly around the way one does in garages. I went to Jive. He bounced and whined his greeting and was happy to be scratched behind the ears. I left him. I went around the hood of the car and approached him idly from the other direction. He lunged at me and his teeth clicked very convincingly about three inches short of my shin. I sprang back a goodly distance and he showed me a demon-face, head tilted, eyes slitted, ears laid back, lips lifted to display very white and businesslike fangs. He snarled a continuous and convincing threat. Experimentally, I went around the front of the car again, and, from that side, got the warmest of greetings. I repeated it experimentally at least eight times, canceling out any possibility of mistake. The little group of service employees who had gathered to watch the show shook their heads and clucked and said the dog was crazy. One of them tried it, but Jive was willing to savage him no matter what direction he came from and indeed began to get so agitated that I had to put a halt to the game. Had he broken that leash, I think he would have emptied that garage in microseconds.

I took him home and told Dorothy it was foolishness to try to live with an animal so erratic. She was saddened by the decision. She hates to have to give up where any living thing is involved. We took him back to Dr. Sellman, who gave him a massive injection of Nembutal, one that took him into a deep sleep and, in ten minutes or so, into death.

Dr. Sellman brought us out the leash and harness and asked if we cared to take a look at the mad dead dog. We declined. No charge, he said, for the execution.

Johnny seemed subdued about it, but quite reasonable, and willing to accept the necessity for it. I suspect that the vivid memory of having been bitten in the mouth tempered his sense of loss. And all other losses had to be measured against the loss of Toppy, she of the eager whiskers, and then the sudden gathering of the flies at the summer roadside. It was easier to say good-by to Jive.

TWO

———————

It was an old and shabby neighborhood, those few blocks along State Street between Oneida Square and the knitting mills. But our windows looked out at the leaves of the old elms, and Dorothy had redecorated that upstairs apartment into a cheerful brightness.

It had one overwhelming advantage. I had decided to try to make our living by writing fiction. We had a few dollars saved, plus my terminal-leave income—four months' pay as a lieutenant colonel. We expected it to be precarious. And that two-bedroom apartment was under rent control, frozen at a monthly rate of $23.50.

State Street sloped downhill toward the mills. The next street down was Mandeville Street, and just around the corner on Mandeville was the Mandeville Market, owned and operated by Howard Ehrenspeck, a good friend then and now. He and Jenny are now over on the east coast of Florida, where Howard is in the insurance business. Once upon a time, when food was half today's cost, he let a very nervous and insecure writer run up a grocery bill of three hundred dollars. People came from all the best parts of the city to trade there. Howard and his employees had been most kind to Dorothy and Johnny. And so it got to be a pleasant habit to take a break and walk over to the market to get a pack of cigarettes and have a soft drink.

That was the way I happened to meet George. At the time I met her, George was one very busy female cat, providing for some six kittens in the basement of the market. George had huge paws. She had six toes on one front foot and seven on the other.

George had her litter in early September in the cellar under the Mandeville Market, in an old grocery carton of her choosing. I met her in October when she was in the process of weaning them. The market was renowned for the quality of the meat. There was a huge chopping block, scrubbed pale, curved to a shallow concavity by long use. There was sawdust on the floor behind the meat counter. On the floor against the back wall near the doorway to the walk-in cooler was the scrap basket, a bushel basket lined with butcher paper into which the meat cutters tossed the trimmings.

The cellar door was propped ajar a few inches, enough room for George to come through. A cellar window was fixed the same way to give George access to the outdoor world, for night ventures and the pursuit of status.

The first time I saw George, she came from the direction of the cellar with an air of purpose, went directly to the scrap basket, hoisted her front feet up onto the rim, and stared down into it, studying the contents. Next, braced by her left front paw, she used the hooks on her right paw to sort down through the scraps of meat. She was very intent and much like a housewife at a melon bin. When at last she found the piece suitable for her children, she leaned in delicately, picked it up in her jaws, reared around and walked back to the cellar stairs with it. Howard told me that sometimes she would come up, sort through the basket, find nothing suitable, give them all a brief, icy glance, and go on back down. And then some very tasty scraps would be tossed into the basket to await her next shopping mission.

George was diligent in the acceptance of her responsibilities. She did not seem to feel that the scrap basket was in any sense a handout. It was there, and because she was doing her part without sloth or complaint, she expected it to be maintained adequately. She was pleased to have people clump down into the cellar and admire the kittens. She would purr extravagantly. A meat-market cat is not inclined toward a pessimistic view of humans. The kittens were lively and healthy.

Not long thereafter Dorothy came walking home from the market with a male kitten from the litter. She was quite tentative about it. We were dog people. If anybody objected, he could be returned to George. She had gone down to the cellar and picked the one most responsive. She said that after such hideous luck with dogs lately, maybe . . .

I was dubious. I had the cat-lovers tagged. There were four categories. The traditional lonely spinster, of course. And that strange clan of hard-jawed, intensely competitive female who breeds for show purposes cats who look like squirrels, monkeys, Pekingese dogs—like almost anything except a cat-cat. Also the eerie eccentric with eleven million dollars in tin cans and pillow slips, who lives in rancid squalor, scavenges trash cans, and keeps thirty-one cats. Lastly the slender-wristed chap with some esoteric relation to the arts, who plays a recorder, decorates with monk's cloth and chicken wire, seats guests on the floor, and buys tinned breast of chicken for his cat.

Kittens were always fine. Mature cats had always seemed to me to be almost spectacularly unrewarding. Prince had despised them.

But perhaps I felt a little guilty about cats. Long ago I had been an apprentice assassin. Or possibly the better phrase would be timid accessory. It happened in Sharon, Pennsylvania. Perhaps I was nine years old. We lived at 215 South Oakland Avenue. My father worked for the Standard Tank Car Company. I knew a boy named Ralph, who lived a block away. He was not a friend. He was twelve years old. That age difference put him well out of the reach of friendship.

I was awed by him. He seemed very large and constructed in a crude and ominous way. He had big hands, big knuckles, a great many large, yellowish teeth, and a raw-boned, shambling, go-to-hell manner. He had the reputation of being a dangerous and merciless fighter. He was hero-villain, the ambivalent image. The only attentions I had ever received from him were unexpected punches on the arm upon the brick-paved playground of the public school. He had developed the knack of hitting at just the right angle and just the right place—about an inch below the point of the shoulder—in such a way it would deaden the entire arm for an hour. When the numbness went away, the ache would begin. He created an entire legion of smaller boys who always revolved slowly when they stood in one place, to prevent anyone drifting up behind them. Ralph had an unwashed smell, an exceptionally pungent vocabulary, and a seemingly perpetual post-nasal drip, which he turned to advantage with a startling WHONK sound, followed by a wha-THOO of deadly accuracy.

Under normal circumstances we would have never shared any exploit, be that the word for caticide (felinicide?). But one weekend afternoon in the early fall, after school had begun again, on my way to find my standard pack of friends, I ran into Ralph walking alone toward the viaduct carrying a black cat in his arms, a mature cat which did not seem completely enchanted by being toted along by Ralph. I imagine he felt the need to explain such an effete act as cat-carrying, and he told me gruffly he was taking this old cat down into the viaduct to teach it how to hunt stuff. Did I want to come along?

I must explain the viaduct. It was a natural gorge which ran through that residential part of town. A bridge crossed it at South Oakland Avenue. It was respectably deep there, a small stream winding along the bottom of it. It had, I know now, a potential natural beauty, but it suffered the abuse one would expect in a small industrial city. People threw junk into it. Kids set fires. I remember the familiar commands: You stay off that bridge, you hear me? Stay out of the viaduct. There are terrible old drunken bums down in those bushes.

The viaduct wandered down the slope toward town and then broadened out into a trashy, cindery area before it reached the railroad yards. I was delighted to be asked to go anywhere with Ralph. It was a status situation. It entitled me to shamble and whonk and say bad words and wish I were not forced to bathe so frequently.

We approached the steep bank after traversing the cinder alley that ran behind the houses on the other side of South Oakland from ours. (It ran behind Brindle's house, the one right across the street from ours. I was in love with Carribelle Brindle, and later with Doris King, and later with Florence Heintz, but we moved away when I was ten years old, before I had a chance to acquaint them with this emotional condition.)

The cat, uneasy enough at level transit, became agitated when we went sliding and scrambling down the steep slope to creek level. At that time in that culture it was pronounced crick. Wash was pronounced warsh. Forty years later I sometimes hear myself revert.

As we reached the creek the cat made some convulsive efforts to escape. Ralph had hold of it firmly, but it hooked him. When he shifted his grasp, it bit him. It bit him on the thumb. He roared and yelled son-of-a-bitch and hurled the cat into the center of a natural pool. The creek entering and leaving the pool was only about three feet across and quite shallow. The pool was an irregular oval perhaps thirty feet across and forty feet long, three or four feet deep in the middle, with a gently sloping shore all the way around it. The tall trees that grew down in the viaduct were leafed out still, the leaves just beginning to change. The afternoon was sunny and cool. There was a city around us, but we were out of sight, as completely as we would have been in a virgin wilderness.

The cat disappeared in the middle and popped up at once, swimming strongly. Ralph raced around to the place where it was planning to emerge. The cat wanted no more association with people. It turned around and headed back across the pool. At Ralph's command I ran and headed it off. At first it required agility because the cat was making good time, but it was expending energy at a dangerous rate and was soon swimming so slowly we could almost saunter to the estimated landing point. "Going to drown him," Ralph announced.

Immediately I lost my stomach for the game. It had been just a game, a curious form of tag. I would like to say that I made violent objection, that I put forward good arguments in favor of mercy, even that I made an attempt to rescue the cat. But this was Ralph, a *big* boy, a whonker, an arm numb-er, a celebrity in my small culture. Protest was as unthinkable as was going away and leaving him there. I backed off a little way and watched with a sickly fascination.

By then the cat's anxiety to avoid Ralph was less than its need to reach land. Looking half asleep, moving quite slowly, it would swim right to Ralph's feet. He wore what was then called hightops, those tough shoes which came to just below the knee, were laced with rawhide, and came with a buckhorn pocketknife which fit into a little snap-fastener pocket on the outside of the right calf. I seemed to have a hundred reasons for feeling inadequate those days. One was that my feet were too tender for those shoes. When wet they stiffened, and one attempt had given me such horrible blisters upon blisters in the futile attempt to swagger rather than limp in them that my mother said never again.

He did not kick the cat. When it came crawling onto the shale, he would gently work the toe of his hightop under its belly, get it in balance, then project it out into the center of the pool. It returned many many times. The cat made no sound. Ralph made no sound. I merely stood and watched. What seemed most curious to me was the way that the cat, with the entire shore line to choose from, came right toward Ralph every time. Possibly in that extremity of its exhaustion, it thought that half-seen figure was help rather than death. It was eerie to see and to remember later, the way it returned to him. Finally, when slung back, it made some aimless motions and then was quite still, turning slowly in the movement of the current through the pond. This was my look at death, the soaked black fur, the scrawny, irreversible stillness.

"Guess we taught that son-of-a-bitch not to bite," Ralph said.

Indeed we did. He wanted to leave it there. I said I

thought burial would be nice. My conscience was beginning to require something. He was patronizingly tolerant. We threw stones to wash it close enough to reach with a branch. He dragged it by the tail to soft ground. I began digging with a stick. Ralph lost interest and wandered off. I hastened the ceremony, prodding the cat into the hole before it was deep enough, then covering it with a hasty layer of dirt, leaves and small stones. I hastened after Ralph and caught up with him when he was halfway up the steep slope. I walked along the alley with him.

"What are you going to do now?" I asked him.

He stopped and gave me a look of total contempt. "Look. You wanna follow me around all day? Stop following me, kid."

I went home through Brindle's yard. I do not remember weeping about that cat. I remember that night in bed feeling soiled, sick, and unworthy. The heroes in my books would never have permitted it. All I could do was wish I had left the house five minutes earlier or later, and then I would never have met him with the cat. I could remember too vividly the early chances I had to let the cat escape. I could have fallen down on purpose. But I couldn't kid myself. That cat knew there were two of us. I knew there were two of us.

I do not know whether it left any mark at all on Ralph. It left a mark on me which has lasted forty years. Not that I am innocent of subsequent crimes of omission. We accumulate remorses the way sea creatures build their shells, so that at last the carapace is an armor, protecting the tender parts from the minor wound. But that was the first time I had faulted my own image through silence, and that was the first time I had realized that death is not a saccharine sleep, but the horrid silence of forever, a black smear of fur in green water.

Now there was a kitten in the house, and a faint uneasiness in me because I had forfeited an obligation to the entire race of Cat.

(There is another cat somewhere in memory, a country kitten which I think my sister Dorrie had for a time. I see it only as a cat half-grown, absurdly clad in doll clothes,

27

sidling apprehensively away from the game, looking back with patient, depressed anxiety, stumbling over skirts and sleeves.)

Kittens are fine. And, like very small children, anonymous. They use the big muscles, are endlessly curious, play the games of run and pounce and pretend, are either violently active or deeply asleep. When healthy and unafraid, they are enchanting, batting the victim spool about with a comedy ferocity, climbing into a lap for the drugged, trusting sleep.

As I accepted the underfoot reality of kitten, I had no intimation that one day, in a curious symbolism, in perhaps an act of cancellation or a reprieve, I would have to kill another black cat, and, in killing him in a manner more grotesque than any invented scene, rid myself of the last guilt about the drowning.

I have no idea why we named the kitten Roger. Perhaps it was out of a mutual impatience with precious names for kittens. Or terribly clever names. Or lit'ry allusions. Or folksy names. Roger seemed a name with an acceptable dignity. He had been weaned on scraps from meat eventually served on the best tables in town. His mother had personal dignity. At the time we knew two Rogers, one a banker and one an attorney, and though he was not named *after* either of them, perhaps their status conditioned our choice of name.

Roger had inherited George's tendency to a multiplicity of toes. Twenty-six, to be precise—six apiece in front, seven in back. He was tiger, black markings on gray, with white feet, a white bib, belly, and muzzle, a nose that started pink and remained pink except for one small brown spot near one nostril. This nose later provided a reliable color-clue to the state of his health. When he is the sickest, it fades to a pink so pale it is almost white.

Tiger markings on house cats are curiously consistent throughout history. And the same markings occur all over the world. The most ancient drawings show this same racial camouflage, the striped alternations of dark and light that, at dawn or dusk, can make the animal almost invisible in a grassy field. The black guard hairs make a line down the spine. The faint dark pattern wrinkles the forehead, stripes the cheeks in a way which seems to make the eyes more expressive, and rings the tail and legs.

We did not know that Roger—and his half brother—would become exceptionally large cats—fourteen pounds and better during their hardiest years—so large that visitors would stare at them and inquire what breed they might be. We learned to say that they were pure Mandeville. But such pretention eventually came to seem a little too smart-ass, so we re-established their dignity by saying the breed was alley cat.

In these days of the huge fluorescent basketry of the supermart, the grocery store is no longer the prime source of house cats. Yet, up until a few years ago, Syd Solomon, the painter, who lives ten minutes away from us in Sarasota, devised a system of his own invention which for a time reversed this trend. He and Annie had several cat families living in their compound on the shore of Philippi Creek. Being naturally squeamish over the chore of bagging up new litters and drowning them in the creek, Syd would don an old hunting jacket with huge pockets, put kittens in the pockets, and go grocery shopping at Marables Market down on Osprey Avenue. The trade there was, and still is, both social and affluent. It is a supermarket. Syd would find an empty aisle, set a kitten down, and hastily walk away. Minutes later a woman would come across the little thing mewling along in confusion, after several more resolute women had passed it by, and her heart would be touched. Ah, the pore little *thing*. The *pore* little darling thing! She would pick it up, ask where it had come from, and, of course, neither the staff nor Eddie Marable would have the faintest idea, and she would take it home. One suspects a wide-flung cat dynasty in south Sarasota and on the keys. Pure Philippi? Or pure Marable. (Pronounced marra-belle)

In the spring of 1946 Dorothy came home from the Mandeville Market with a kitten from George's next litter. Two cats are better than one. Their reaction to each other adds an extra dimension of cat-watching. Then would not three be better than two? I do not think so. I think that at three and beyond they tend to set up a social order which diminishes the importance to them of their relationship with humans, and thus lose a certain responsiveness, tending more to become cat's cats rather than people's cats, In other terms, the cat by instinct tends to establish itself with a co-operative living arrangement known as a pride when one speaks of lions. With proper trust established, the cat will make the unnatural adjustment of accepting the huge, two-legged beasts as members of the pride. Two cats will accept and confirm this disparate relationship, but when there are three or more there is enough quantity for the formation of the instinctive community which can then consider the nearby humans as bond servants, furniture, and infrequent sources of clumsy entertainment.

Roger spent about thirty seconds reacting to the newcomer as though it might be an exceptionally large and dangerous bug. Roger was beginning to be a boy cat, rangier and more agile. We could not guess what his response would be. He astonished us by becoming almost idiotically maternal. He washed the kitten day after day into a strangely sodden state. He was almost consistently gentle with it, enduring its fierce little needle-toothed games, but sometimes his own kittenhood would get out of control, and he would bat the little fur ball across the kitchen floor until it yelled with consternation and alarm.

I remember how we named the new one. I had a dictionary with lists of first names in the back. We went through the list of male names to find one which might fit properly with Roger. We did not have to go very far down the list. To Dorothy, to Johnny, and to me the name Geoffrey had precisely the right ring.

A different tom had fathered that spring litter. In vastly oversimplified terms, Roger was a long blue cat and Geoff was a square brown cat. It never failed to astonish us that some people had difficulty telling them apart.

Geoffrey became a chunky cat, his shoulders and forearms considerably more massive than Roger's. His face was broader, forehead higher, nose dark. The short fur on his face had a definite red-brown tinge. His ears had lynx tufts Roger's did not. His belly fur had a pale buff tinge. The shape of his jowls was more leonine. Roger's head configuration can best be described by saying that sometimes he is known as Old Turtle-head. Where the line of Geoff's back was quite straight, Roger's narrow hind quarters stand higher than his shoulders. People who despise cats always found it easier to despise Roger, even though—if it is the distillation of catness they so instinctively fear—Geoff was the more primitive, the one ever more aware of the obligations of his profession.

All three of us were, I must confess, thinking of these cats as temporary. Not that we had any idea of disposing of them, but rather because we had the dual pessimism of thinking that something always happens to cats—and something always happens to our animals. We had the feeling cats are temporary despite the example of Nicky, a husky, square, black and white, businesslike cat owned by Dorothy's paternal grandmother in Poland, New York. Nicky was then in his teens, and, whether he was at home at the old house in Poland, or up at the family cottage at Piseco Lake in the summer, it was his nightly habit to slay his quota of rodents—moles, shrews, mice—and place them in a curiously neat array on the porch, side by side, heads all pointing in the same direction. Nicky, a mighty hunter, had elected himself provider and made it his business to forage for his pride, his community. That the offerings were not accepted in the spirit they were acquired made no difference to him. He had all the quiet confidence of a master woodsman.

We knew of Nicky's durability but thought of him as an exception. Our cats would not last as long. We were sure of that.

Dorothy brought them home, and they became a part of life. As we were on the second floor, and traffic was heavy on State Street, and dogs prowled the neighborhood, we did not let them out. They quickly accepted the shallow box filled with newspaper torn into strips. When they were more sure-footed, we let them out onto a small flat area of the roof, too high for jumping.

I was involved in the desperate business of trying to wrest a living out of free-lance fiction for magazines. The first story, written while overseas, had sold to Whit Burnett for *Story* Magazine. During those first four months of effort, I wrote about 800,000 words of unsalable manuscript, all in short-story form. That is the equivalent of ten average novels. Writing is the classic example of learning by doing. Had I done a novel a year, it would have taken me ten years to acquire the precision and facility I acquired in four months. I could guess that I spent eighty hours a week at the typewriter. I kept twenty-five to thirty stories in the mails at all times, sending each of them out to an average of ten potential markets before retiring them.

Except for Dorothy, everyone thought I was a readjustment problem. Even today I do not know how much of her confidence in me was genuine and how much was a calculated effect devised for my morale. But I do know that her attitude was that it would be absurd to think of spending my life in any other way.

In the fifth month, in February of 1946, I sold my second story. For forty dollars. It brought my lifetime earnings from writing up to a total of sixty-five dollars. I had a wife, a son, two cats—and almost one thousand form letters of rejection.

But as this account is of cats rather than of writing, let me say that by the last day of 1946, the total was over six thousand dollars, and we were living in the Hill Country of Texas, in Ingram ("The Only All Rock Town in the U.S.") in a hillside cabin.

THREE

I have no patience with those crypto-primitives—who are almost invariably of the moneyed leisure class—who seem to believe there is something effete or degrading to the animal in altering a male house cat.

The tomcat is a damned nuisance. He pursues his specialty to the almost complete exclusion of other interests. His is a nocturnal existence so rigorous, he spends his days flaked out, stirring once in a while to go see if anybody has put anything in his dish. He shreds upholstery in the serious business of keeping his claws and shoulder muscles in fighting trim. He develops a voice which will shatter glassware at twenty paces. His eerie howls of challenge disturb the neighborhood. He roams far and is sometimes gone for days in a row, returning sated, surly, smug, and bearing the wounds of love and combat. He stakes out his territory with extraordinarily pungent little driblets of urine, and will occasionally stake out the house where he lives, either just for the hell of it or because another animal has been there during his absence. Owning a tomcat is curiously akin to working in some menial capacity for one of the notorious Lotharios of show business.

On the other hand, waiting too long to fix a cat results in an end product equivalently unattractive. The hormones have had too much chance to alter body chemistry, and then when the animal is deprived of this source, its physical adjustment is to become a eunuch cat, fat, slow, sedentary, sleepy, and not at all playful. A glutton cat, inclined to flatulence and timidity.

The ideal, in view of the ultimate personality of the cat, is to have him castrated just as soon as the testicles are sufficiently apparent to make it possible. Body chemistry will not have altered. He will remain lithe and active. He will be responsive and retain some portion of the psychology of his kittenhood all his life. And, as this account will show, he will not be cowardly or lack a sense of adventure. The younger the cat the more minor the operation and the quicker the recovery. We took them in turn, waited, brought them home. They were cross and slightly baleful for about one day.

Roger lost his tomhood before one of his secondary sex characteristics had time to develop. He never has acquired an adult cat voice. Except in combat, or just before he vomits, Roger has a kitten mew, an entirely futile device for getting doors opened or his dish filled. In the stress of war or nausea, he can make ululations rather like a drunken lyric soprano with the croup.

Geoffrey achieved mature vocal chords. There is a curious sidelight to this difference in voice. As we have always followed the sun, there have always been screened doors. We have always arranged a window with cat shelves fastened to the outside of houses so the cats could come and go as they pleased. But sometimes their window would be closed. Roger soon learned to beat on the outside of the screen doors with his fists, making a racket like that off-stage thunder achieved by shaking a piece of sheet metal. For about the first six years of his life, Geoffrey took the traditional approach of sitting outside the door and bellowing for it to be opened. Sometimes they would both be out there, one thumping and one shouting. I would judge each method equally effective.

But quite suddenly Geoff switched to Roger's system. He was six years old. He was in fine voice. It is impossible to guess what manner of reasoning was involved. Certainly he did not give up the use of his voice for other demands. In fact, he perfected it. During his last years, possibly through trial and error, he finally achieved the ultimate effectiveness in demanding food. I can define it only as an abrupt, abused, stentorian whine. Human nerve ends could take no more than thirty seconds of that. It could have been stupendously effective in getting doors opened. But he knocked on doors, as his brother did.

There was one sound they made which was almost identical, Roger's just slightly weaker and pitched a few notes higher. It is a distinctive and recognizable sound all cats use. It means, "Where are you?" It means, "Come and play." Ah-*rowr?* Ah-*rowr?* Ah-*rowr?* The accent is on the second syllable, which ends on a rising inflection. There is two- to three-second pause between each questioning call. If humans and cats are indeed part of the same pride, they will call humans and can be called by them with this portion of the standard vocabulary, though generally it is a cat-to-cat affair. They quickly become skeptical of people who go around making too many cat noises. So do I.

While we were still on State Street and the cats were small, an acquaintance named Hank sat in the kitchen and deliberately broke the end of Roger's tail about three or four vertebrae from the tip. I do not remember exactly what brief high-level conversation preceded it, something like, "You wanna see how you can make a cat make a hell of a funny noise?" And before anyone could object he had reached and pinched the end of Roger's tail. Roger made a sound ranging from the top limits of audibility right up into supersonic range and ran in place for several seconds until he got enough traction on the linoleum to scoot off into the other room. Hank chuckled merrily. We did not know he had broken the tail at that time. Apparently he got the tail between the thumb and the first two fingers, held the fingers a little apart, and pinched the tail into the open space.

I am glad that we did not know. We let it be known quite forcefully that we saw nothing funny about hurting a cat. (Or about picking up beagle pups by their ears.) But Hank acted as if we were very odd people. I know he did not do it out of willful cruelty. The world is full of Hanks. They know that animals are living creatures, but their knowledge is not in any way subjective. Impoverished in some curious way, they have no empathy toward animal pain, and cannot really understand why other people do not feel just as they do. It puzzles them, because they feel no lack within themselves.

It would have done no good to have ordered Hank out of the house or to have made any attempt to explain to him.

For some time thereafter Roger did not care to have anyone touch his tail. Perhaps a month later, with Roger once again tolerant about tail-touching, Dorothy called to me in some astonishment and had me come and feel of the cat's tail. About an inch and a half from the tip it angled off at about a twenty-degree angle. His fur concealed this little bend. The angle of the bend was fixed and rigid. Suddenly we both remembered Hank and realized for the first time the tail had been broken and had healed in this fashion.

It did not seem to bother Roger. He could lash the tail. He could carry it high as a banner when registering affection, twining around the legs of the people. And, unlike Geoff at that time, he had given up the kid stuff of suddenly chasing it, grabbing the tip, tumbling over and over with it.

Geoff, otherwise sedate in so many ways, chased the tip of his own tail all his life. It was a very infrequent game. You would hear a scrabbling, scurrying sound and look down, and there on the linoleum would be Geoff whirling in solemn frenzy. He even did it once during the weeks he was enfeebled by the sickness he died of, at fourteen. On a day when he was feeling a little better, he performed the solitary celebration of catching that elusive tail.

Roger's broken tail did serve in a functional and handy

way for years. When you came upon one of them in the dark, you had only to finger the tip of the tail to make the quickest and most efficient identification of which one you had.

Ten years later, in Sarasota, I came home from some errand one afternoon, and Dorothy announced that Roger had lost his tail. My immediate mental picture was considerably eased when I saw the cat and saw that he had lost that inch or so beyond the old break. The loss did not enhance his already dwindling beauty. He seemed to have no trauma, in fact no awareness he had become, overall, a shorter cat. The tail looked squared off, with the squared end unpleasantly ragged. This was no discernible wound, no infection. I believe that circulation eventually ceased beyond the break. The nerves were dead, probably, from the time of the break. The tip atrophied and finally dropped off.

A little later I saw Dorothy going slowly by the windows outside, staring at the ground, a thoughtful expression on her face. When she came in I asked her what she was doing, she said she was searching for Roger's tail. She never found it.

Within a matter of weeks the way the hair grew at the end of the truncated tail changed completely, forming itself into the same glossy terminal tip as before. No one could guess it had ever been longer.

I have talked of the hurting of animals, and because this book is about the relationship between cats and people, I should at least make mention of our ambivalent attitude in these matters, though I have no hope of explaining it. I do not hunt. We do not kill snakes. Dorothy carries housebound bugs into the great outdoors for release but is pure hell on a clothes moth. We trap whitefoot mice in our Adirondack camp and hate doing it. We both enjoy sports fishing. And we are both aficionados of the bull ring. Were the horses unpadded, we wouldn't be. I am not interested in arguing these inconsistencies with anyone.

As Geoff became less helpless, Roger gave him an increasingly hard time. Right in the midst of washing him,

Roger would bite him. Geoff would squall and run, and when Roger came bounding after him, Geoff would roll onto his back and defend himself from that position. It set the pattern for all the rest of their time together. Geoff would always yell as though he were being savaged to death. When he was the smaller we would separate them when it seemed to get too rough. Eventually we learned, after they were of a size, that Geoff's vocalized anguish was part of the game. And he started as many incidents as did Roger.

For years their most predictable time of play-battle was in the morning while we were having breakfast. After a certain amount of chase and flight, it always settled into the same pattern, Geoff on his back, paws ready for defense, while Roger, ears laid back, would make half circles around him, getting ever closer, looking for the chance to either spring in and take a nip at some unprotected place and bounce back out of range, or to find a major advantage, a moment of unwariness, and come piling on, going for the neck, while Geoff would apparently try to disembowel him with his hind claws. You could hear the thuds as they hit each other with their paws. Little tufts of torn hair would drift in the morning sunlight. And Geoffrey would scream of murder being done. Never once were their roles in this mock battle reversed. Roger attacked; Geoff defended. As they grew older the invitations to battle became more considerate and ceremonial. No longer did one or the other crouch in hiding and spring upon the unwary. The victim cat might not be in the mood. An explosive exhalation, more huff than hiss, was adequate warning to stay the hell off. The rejected cat would walk away, sit, and begin to wash. This indicates awareness of a social error. It is the cat response to inadvertently falling, or being laughed at, or being slung off a chair, or letting a mouse escape. A man might start a tuneless little whistle and rock on his heels and fiddle with his necktie and stare into space. Cats go a little distance away and sit and start grooming themselves, starting with a few licks at the shoulder, never glancing back toward the place where the humiliation occurred.

As they matured, the invitation to the game was expressed by washing the face and neck of the other cat and, during this process, chancing the tentative bite. If there was no response, the cat making the query could save face by continuing the washing chore as though nothing had happened. If the nip was returned, the game was on.

As they changed from all the anonymous energies of kittenhood into the gangling specifics of teen-age cats, their personalities and their reactions to people became increasingly perceptible and distinct.

Roger wanted all relationships to be on his terms. He despised being picked up, and would begin a struggling that increased in intensity until he was put down. He would let you know when he wanted to be stroked, and then his engine-voice acceptance of it was a kind of gluttony. He was incomparably stubborn, egocentric, overconfident, often vile-tempered. But of the two he had the greater curiosity, and figured things out more quickly.

Geoff was more placid. He accepted what seemed to be expected of him at any time. He was content to be held. There were always children in the house, Johnny and his friends, visiting nephews, children of our friends. I wonder how many times we said, "The one with the white face will bite." Roger would play with the kids, but when the game got to be a little too much, there would come that venomous huff, claws unsheathed, the ears laid back, and too often the yelp of a scratched child before Roger stalked away. Geoff never once bit or scratched a child, though I can remember once seeing him being used as a sort of roller under a sturdy small boy, with enough pressure on him, I swear, to make his eyes bulge. When Geoff had enough he would quietly and persistently disentangle himself and go away and hide. He seemed to trust children in a way Roger apparently found incomprehensible. Roger did not trust anyone too much but preferred adults.

In some gradual and unplanned way, Roger became "my" cat, and Geoff became Johnny's. Perhaps Roger and I shared some kindred abrasive quality in our personalities. I seemed to intrigue him, particularly when I tormented him in minor ways. Some of these torments became ritual games between us. I will tell of these later on.

Dorothy fixed up an office for me in a very small room

off the living room. It was about seven by nine, with one window, and had been some sort of clothes closet and storage room. It got me out of the dining room where, after school hours, small-fry traffic was dense. Roger became my office cat, sprawled atop a low file cabinet, sleeping and watching me by the hour. When he felt the need of a little action he would hop over to my desk and start batting things off onto the floor deliberately. But he did not do this often enough for any serious nuisance value. I think it was at that time I began to think of old Turtlehead as a kind of mascot. We had acquired him during the first full month I tried to write for a living. Things were beginning to move and pay off. Possibly writers are as superstitious as baseball players or circus performers. All three professions are concerned with the interaction of skill and luck, and to both ballplayers and writers, slump is one of the truly horrid words in the language.

Though Roger did not care to be held, he vastly enjoyed riding around on anyone's shoulder. I learned the wisdom of making no sudden moves or turns. Twenty-six claws can anchor a cat very solidly.

Roger's joy in being toured about the house in this manner led to one interesting discovery. Morning or evening, when you were bent over the bathroom lavatory brushing your teeth, Roger delighted in leaping from the floor to your back, landing high on the back of one shoulder or the other. If your back was bare, he would land with uncanny lightness and delicacy, without a claw protruding. Yet if you wore just one covering of fabric, no matter how light, he would land with all claws seeking purchase. This could be such an unforgettable experience, we all became bareback toothbrushers.

Johnny toted Geoff about endlessly, a limp, happy, purring bundle of adoration. There was one aspect of this which seems contrary to instinct. If Geoff started to slip he would not grab with his claws to prevent falling. He would just keep on slipping, in total confidence that he would be grabbed and hiked back up where he belonged.

In their very walks the two cats seemed to express the variations in personality. Roger's front legs were bowed. He placed one front paw in direct line with the previous

40

step. (Now, in old age, this has become so exaggerated that there is an actual overlap, the right foot being placed further to the left than the left foot will be on the next step. It is a strange, cross-legged gait.) This, plus the greater length of his hind legs and the consequent height of his rear end, gave him a very slinking gait, and he looked constantly from side to side, as though pretending to be a tiger on the prowl.

Geoffrey trudged. He also inherited the excess-toe gene, and he had five in back but two extra ones on each front foot placed high enough to give sort of a dew-claw effect. Unlike Roger, the extra toes seemed to give Geoffrey's feet a curious lumpiness which altered his gait. He trudged along on straight legs, making more of a thumping sound than one properly expects from a cat. He did not look to right or left. His forehead markings gave him a visible frown. He seemed always to be headed on some somber errand requiring concentration.

For a long time I could not imagine why Geoffrey's walk was so comically unlike the walk of any cat I had ever seen. Then one day I noticed what it was. Roger and every other cat I have ever observed have been trotters— moving both legs on one side alternately, so that when the right front is extended ahead, the right rear is extended out behind, and the feet on the left side are closest together. Geoff was a pacer, moving the legs on each side in unison.

Despite the stolid lack of grace in Geoff's walk, he had the greater precision and agility in feats of—excuse the expression—catrobatics. When Roger was old enough to have known better, we have seen him try to chase a small object under a couch too low for him and give himself such a ringing crack on the skull that he rebounded, dazed and glazed. And then walk unsteadily away to sit and wash and contemplate space. Geoff was never that clumsy. Roger, in mad dashes through the household, was always the one who knocked things over.

And when, finally, they became outdoor cats, Geoff was the hunter. Roger had a desperate desire to catch things, and he tried very hard, but the wildlife seemed almost to laugh at him. I shall tell later of the adventures of the hunt.

41

When Dorothy's brother, Sam Prentiss, and his wife, Evelyn, and their two small boys visited us that year, they decided Mandeville cats were giving birth to litters of very superior kittens. And so they obtained one. Apparently that litter had been fathered by the same tom who fathered Roger. Their male kitten was built very much like Roger, though of slightly better configuration. Like Roger he grew to be a big, long cat. His coat was a strange and beautiful lavender shade of gray. He had extra toes.

They named him Mittens. But as his personality became more evident, it soon became apparent that such a name was like calling Caligula sweetums. When it came to baleful, he made Roger look like a buttercup. His early years were incomparably surly. After making his acquaintance during a joint vacation at Piseco Lake I renamed him Heathcliffe, and the name stuck. He lived to be seventeen. In his later years when, as in the case of Roger, he adopted an astonishing benignity as a way of life, it became Heathie. Curiously enough, sold on our theory of two cats being the optimum quantity, they acquired a gray tiger named Charlie in the Albany area where they still live, and Charlie turned out to be the same sort of sturdy, amiable, loving type as Geoff.

A final note about George. We had discovered that Geoffrey could use the larger dewclaw on his front right foot much as an opposed thumb. We kept his catnip in a glass jar with a mouth just wide enough for him to stick his hand in. Roger would reach in, claw catnip out, and lap it off the floor. Geoffrey would reach in, curl his paw around a wad of catnip, hold it in place with the opposed thumb, and then eat it out of the palm of his hand, looking oddly monkeylike during the process. We had him demonstrate this talent to many visitors, and often the subsequent conversation became quite fanciful, speaking of Geoffrey as an example of a feline mutation which, in time, might lead to the use of tools and the consequent increase in adaptive intelligence. Yet if he was a mutation, he had been deprived of the chance of passing this gene along to future generations of cats.

At about this time George, between litters, was run over and killed one night on Mandeville Street near the store.

With her died the chance of more males with prehensile toes, a trait they could pass along, if left their tomishness.

Cats, so survival-prone in almost all other ways, are pathetically stupid about highways. At night they become too intense about the hunt and about sex and apparently feel so fleet they believe nothing can touch them as they streak across. They make a sorry and inconsequential little thud against a front tire.

Incidentally, Geoffrey was the only cat we have ever seen make an observable adjustment to the highway problem. In 1951 we were in a rented house on Casey Key, between Sarasota and Venice. We were at a narrow part of the key. The frame cottage was on the bay side. The unpaved road went between the house and the beach. When we went over to the beach, the cats would often go with us. Our shell path stopped at the edge of the road, then continued on the other side.

Time after time we would see Geoffrey come along the path, trudge, trudge, trudge. He would come to a complete stop right at the edge of the road. He would look to the left and then to the right. These were not hasty glances. They were calm appraisals of the situation. Assured the way was clear, he would trudge on across the road and along the path. We had to keep an eye on Roger. He was a fool about traffic. But after watching Geoff's behavior we did not worry about him.

I think that he was probably hit by a car, a nudge, or a glancing blow which hurt him without injuring him. Being a methodical cat, he could certainly relate cause and effect and did so demonstrably in many other areas during his lifetime.

FOUR

––––––

The winter stay in Texas without the cats requires some explanation. Along in April and May of 1946, though I had begun to sell some stories here and there, they were to pulp magazines, and the money was small. I began to think we might not make it.

I found a job as Executive Director of the Taxpayers' Research Bureau in Utica. I made that jump a little too nervously and hastily. I spent every spare moment writing. Through the summer the stories began to sell at a greater rate and to better markets. We paid off our debts and began to build up a little surplus. By autumn I was still stuck with that job, and with an unwritten obligation to keep it for a year. There we were with the funds and the mobility to evade the misery of a Utica winter. I resigned on the basis of need to take Dorothy to a warmer climate. It was not entirely a pretext. She could have endured the winter, but she does not take cold well, and it was certain that she would spend a good portion of the winter in poor health. We arranged to go to Taos.

Dorothy's long-widowed mother, Rita—pronounced in the Dutch manner, *Right*-a—was living in Poland, New York. It made sense to keep the inexpensive State Street apartment and have Rita move in from Poland for the winter and live there and take care of the cats.

We did not make it to Taos. En route we looked at that Hill Country of Texas north of San Antonio and approved immediately. In the spring Rita became ill, and we had to return before we had planned. We still had our little green prewar Ford convertible with huge mileage on it. We were towing a jeep trailer, an army surplus purchase. At anything over thirty-five miles an hour, the car gobbled both gas and oil. There had been a temporary lull in sales, and we were down to a hundred dollars and no credit cards.

I estimated that if we kept it at thirty-five, and stayed on the road fourteen hours a day, and were circumspect about food and lodging, we could make it in good season on the cash in hand.

We arrived with a little less than ten dollars to find two substantial checks waiting, Rita on the mend, the apartment closed, and the cats boarding at Dr. Sellman's. When we went to get them we found they had ingratiated themselves with the management, and instead of being confined to the normal kennel cage, had the run of the cellar. One can imagine that if the earliest memories are of the damp and darkness of a cellar, that same environment will always be reassuring.

In fact, during all of Geoffrey's life, he had a special thing about cardboard cartons. Roger liked them, but not to the same degree. Nothing could be unpacked without Geoff establishing himself in the empty box moments after it became empty, looking fatuously content. Though when well he was not interested in sleeping in a box, he definitely wanted one when he was sick. He was restless when sick, and a box was the only thing which would stop his roaming from place to place trying to get comfortable. To Roger a box was more of a game place, a place to hide and pounce from. To Geoff it was ancient security.

We took them back to the apartment and they re-explored every corner of it and settled back into their routine.

At just about that time we were dislodged from our low-rent haven. It was still under rent control, but the house was sold, and the new owner elected to move into our apartment. That was the only legal way we could have been cast adrift.

After dreary rounds of overpriced and depressingly gloomy apartments, we decided to buy a house. Believing in our innocence that a small college town might provide a pleasant atmosphere for the writer, we looked extensively around Clinton, New York, near Utica, where Hamilton College is located, and at last found a large and very pleasant house up on the Hill, almost surrounded by college property. It was being sold by a Mr. Prettyman, the Athletic Director, who had built most of it himself and had not gotten around to finishing off the upstairs, a factor that kept it within our rather optimistic price range.

College Hill, that spring, was the cats' introduction to the out of doors at ground level. They were tense and apprehensive. It was one hell of a lot of space for small animals. It was full of unfamiliar scents and shapes. Geoff, though the first to adjust, retained a certain wary conservatism about the potential dangers. Roger, after a few exploratory ventures, became entirely foolhardy. I believe that if a bear had appeared, Roger would have made his typically clumsy attempt at stalking it. He seemed to have that quality of egocentricity which made him think nothing would dare eat him.

It was there that we arranged the first cat window for them. You cut a square hole of sufficient size in a window screen, trim the removed portion down a bit, and hinge it back on with two small pieces of wire. A piece of plywood as tall as the exit and as long as the rest of the window opening keeps too much wind from entering on cool days. To the outside of the house, depending on the height above the ground and the agility of the cats, you affix one or two cat shelves in place with angle irons. It helps to have another at sill level, just outside their exit. On cool days

47

when the sun is just right they will take their ease on the shelves, watching the world from a benign height, knowing the retreat hatch is handy.

Roger came and left in silence. Geoffrey left in silence, but would always announce his return. Rahr? Rahr? He would stump through the house toward us, saying, Geoffrey is here. If that announcement was curiously distorted or muffled, it was wise, we learned, to pay attention. He would have a mouthful of victim.

Dorothy and I have tried to make a reasonably accurate estimate of the number of birds Geoff slew in his lifetime. We think that twenty would be the absolute top, and that ten is a more likely figure. Many of those were killed because he caught them before Dorothy learned a system of taking them away from him. We thought the birds were being mangled, and when we leaped at Geoff with shrill cries of consternation, accusation, and dismay, he would give one emphatic crunch and the bird would be dead. I imagine nothing is more futile than trying to convince a cat he is morally wrong to catch birds.

Soon we discovered that the shocked and bedraggled look of the birds was a product of the actual capture, and that Geoff held them in his mouth with an uncanny delicacy. The curve of the fangs held them in place. He was inflicting no wound or bruise.

The proper procedure was to admire him extravagantly, and in the right tone of voice. Geoff, you are a great cat. Stroke his head. Tell him it is a lovely bird. Then he would, more often than not, lay it down gently. If he did not, you could stroke him again and bring thumb and finger around for gentle pressure on the hinges of the jaw. Then you could pick up the undamaged bird, shocked into immobility, and put it in some high, safe place, usually in a shallow cardboard box atop a car or high hedge or edge of a low roof. After minutes of shock-induced lethargy, the bird would suddenly jump up, stare around, and go rocketing off, yelling about its horrid experience.

The well-fed cat is not terribly interested in eating a bird. And apparently the instinct is to bring the game home undamaged. A few times, a very few times, when we were not at home, Geoff would eat a bird. We would find a few feathers by his dish. He was the methodical cat. If you are going to eat something, you take it to where you always eat, and you eat it there. I think we averaged about ten or fifteen birds a year released undamaged.

We cannot remember Roger ever catching a bird. Maybe he grazed a few. He exhibited extreme nervous enthusiasm when Geoff would bring one home, and the problem was to keep him from falling upon it when Geoff set it down.

There was a considerable difference in their hunting technique. I have watched Roger trying to sneak up on something. He worms along on his belly, ears flat, tail thrashing. I think it was the tail which made him so ineffectual. Secrecy seems improbable when the tail is whacking the grass and the brush. And possibly his breathing was audible. It might have seemed to any bird that a rackety little steam engine was slowly approaching. Roger's proficiency level limited him to bugs and beetles, small hoptoads, the infrequent butterfly, and, on a very few triumphant occasions, a rodent. It would please me to give him credit for one entire rabbit, but the implausibility of it would seem to make Geoffrey the captor and donor.

We were privileged several times to witness Geoff's curious and effective hunting method. I suspect that it was only one of his methods. I believe that it was the result of his lumpy feet, odd gait, and unexpected agility. I think he invented the system, finding that he was not very apt at sneaking up on things.

He would go trudging across the lawn, frowning, staring straight ahead, obviously uninterested in anything around him. His route would take him under small trees. Birds would scold him and, growing bolder, come down into the small trees to cuss him out at close range. One of them would get just a little too close. That solemn, square cat could suddenly, without warning, without even seeming to break stride, go five feet into the air and clap those two front feet onto the abusive bird just as it took off from the limb it had thought safely out of reach. In effect, he was using himself as a lure. Perhaps this system is not unique, but I have never heard of any other cat using it.

Our property was bordered on one side by what was known as the Saunders Strip. This was where a Professor Saunders, a delightful old man with astonishingly young eyes, bred tree peonies in great profusion, huge sizes, and uniquely beautiful colors.

One day Dorothy called me from my typewriter to see what Roger was doing, and there was enough urgency in her voice to bring me on the run. There was Roger in the taller grass of the Saunders Strip beyond our lawn, stalking a magnificent cock pheasant larger than himself. Stalking is not exactly the word. He was following it, using the posture and attitudes of the stalk, about six feet behind it. But the bird was entirely aware of him. It would stop and look back at him with assured, beady malevolence, and Roger would stop. When the bird moved on, he would follow.

It is, of course, totally pointless to call a cat when it is intent on the chase. They are deaf to the interruptive nonsense of humans. They are on cat business, totally serious and involved.

Dorothy called Roger.

He lifted his head, stared toward us, and came bounding out of the field and across the lawn and right to us. Did someone want the cat? Did someone call me? He came when called only when it pleased him to come, and so it could not have been more obvious. That big bird was making him terribly nervous. He had not known how to break off the relationship, how to extricate himself from impasse. He had leaped at this chance of retreat with honor. (Damn it, if they hadn't called me just then, I would have caught that thing, whatever it was.)

One day when there were several adults and a batch of kids out in the driveway, Geoff came walking out of the tall grass in our back lot making a very curious sound. He had a grass snake in his mouth, an extremely active little snake about eighteen inches long and as big around as a lead pencil. He was holding it by the middle, with both ends writhing about. Obviously the taste and texture displeased him, as he had his lips pulled back from his teeth in a fixed sneer of distaste, accounting for the strangeness of the sound he was making.

When he reached the group he put it down immediately and backed away, making little tasting motions, lapping his jaws. Roger was there and witnessed how Geoffrey was commended for skill and valor as the snake fled rapidly off into the grass.

Not five minutes later Roger came out of the grass with a snake of his own. Not the same one. This one was smaller. He came bounding out of the grass, dropped his snake, batted at it a couple of times, and watched it flee. I realize all the dangers of imputing more awareness to these animals than they had. But when Roger sat and began sedately to wash, it was as though he was saying, "See? I'm pretty good at that sort of thing too."

Geoff soon became a very proficient mouser at College Hill. And generally he preferred to eat them. He hardly ever made them the objects of that game humans think so cruel and horrid, of grasp and toss and bat about, almost but never quite permitting escape. He would bring his field mice back to the yard or into the house, and if they tried to leave while he was getting ready to eat, he would make a lightning movement of one paw and hold them down. When he was ready, his precision was surgical—the nip of the spine which killed instantly, the long abdominal slit to permit removal of the tiny gall bladder, and then swift, efficient ingestion.

Once in a while he would let Roger have one of his mice. He would sit then and watch Roger play the horrible game. Roger was not interested in eating them. But there seemed to be two inevitable results. Either he became too rough and inadvertently killed them or in trying to work the narrow escape bit let the mouse genuinely escape. In either event, Geoff would get up and trudge away, as though anxious to disassociate himself from the whole clumsy mess.

This mousing reputation of the younger cat came to the attention of our neighbors on the other side, Professor and Mrs. John Mattingly. There was a small barn behind their house. That year John had constructed a corral and purchased a middle-aged, five-gaited show horse named Blue Genius. We had a small terrace on that side of the house which overlooked the corral. Blue Genius was an incurable ham. When he was aware that he had an audience, he would go around and around the perimeter of his corral, neck arched, springing nicely, exhibiting his gaits. Then he would come to the nearest portion of the railing, stick his head over, blow, and wait for the applause. If the quantity pleased him, he would repeat the whole business.

John asked me if they could enlist the assistance of Geoffrey in ridding the small barn of mice which were eating the grain. I said certainly, and a day or so later he asked if I could bring Geoff over to be introduced to his duties. I did so and found that Professor Mattingly had cut a small and perfect Gothic arch in the sliding door of the barn, about a foot above the bottom sill. He felt we should acquaint the cat with this mode of access. As Geoff was accustomed to the window system, I was certain it would take but one trip in and out through the arch to give him all he needed to know. John went into the barn and closed the door. I passed Geoffrey through. John picked him up and sent him back out through the arch. At John's insistence, we repeated this at least a dozen times. Geoff endured it with his usual obliging stoicism, but I can imagine he must have thought we had both gone mad. After the final passage into the barn, John picked Geoff up and dropped him into a grain bin. There was a scuffle of about two seconds duration, and Geoff arched out of the bin with a mouthful of mouse, leaped handily through his arch, and trotted on home. John was delighted. Thereafter Geoff apparently made it a standard part of his rounds because the mouse trouble diminished slowly to zero.

I shall skip cats for a moment to pay tribute to the Mattinglys. They were childless at that time, and both scholars. He taught Latin and Greek. Her specialty was Sanskrit. It was their habit in good weather, when schedule permitted, to go out onto the hillside behind their property and read to each other. It seemed a charming habit. One day our Johnny was missing so long that we began to worry about him. He came home and when asked where he had been, he said he had been out on the hillside reading to the Mattinglys. He said he had read them a whole book, and showed it to us. It was one of those one-dollar, inch-thick collections of Dagwood and Blondie comic strips. He said they both liked it a lot. It still touches us that those gentle and gracious people should have so politely endured one small boy's intrusion upon their private pleasure.

That summer we were able to take our two-week turn at Wanahoo, Dorothy's family's camp at Piseco Lake, fifty miles northeast of Utica on Route 8. So many branches of the family were sharing the camp, scheduling was tight. Piseco Lake is a part of Dorothy's life and now a part of mine too. The family camp was built in 1878. Dorothy's grandmother used to go there when it was a two-day trip by carriage from Poland, stopping overnight at the inn at Hoffmeister. Dorothy was taken there for the first time when she was three weeks old.

When she was a child her father had tried to buy land on the other side of the lake. There were no camps over there. It was owned by the International Paper Company. While I was in India during the war she wrote me that the paper company had decided to sell that land in two-hundred-foot lake-front pieces, some eight hundred feet deep, extending back to the dirt road called the WPA road. I had just had a very fortunate session at the poker table with some people heavy with flight pay, and I was able to send her a little sheaf of hundred-dollar money orders. She got the other few hundred needed from her brother and bought the land. She and Johnny and the surveyor went back and forth through the woods during the black-fly season, trying to set the lines so they would include the point of land on the lake shore she wanted. Gas rationing kept people from getting up there and buying the land. Our piece was the first sold, and they used our lines as the basing point for all subsequent two-hundred-foot sites east and west of us. By the following morning, after surveying the site, Johnny was an awe-inspiring object. His black-fly bites had puffed him up so that he had no neck at all, a bulging and distended face with a nubbin of a nose and slits for eyes. He looked like a small, expressionless Siberian assassin. He insisted he felt well enough to go to school, so Dorothy walked him to the school nearby so that she could explain to his teacher what had happened and tell her she would come and get him if he felt badly. As she approached the school, holding him by the hand, the other kids out in front stared at him in awe and fell back in silence. They did not even know who he was, or, probably, what he was.

So part of our Piseco time that first summer we took the cats up was to start planning the camp we hoped to put on our land some day. We had learned during the few necessary local trips how loudly and bitterly both cats objected to riding in a car. This was the longest one yet. Twelve miles to Utica, and then (past Toppy's tree) fifty miles to the lake. They made the trip hideous. They complained with every breath. By the time we got there Geoff was down to a breathy baritone rasp.

Cats will travel well if you start them early enough and take them often enough. On our way to Texas we had stopped in Virginia to see my sister, Doris, and her husband, Bill Robinson. Bill was getting an engineering degree at V.P.I. They had a black female cat named Buckethead. When they started the gypsy existence of a civil engineer, Buckethead traveled well. They had a sandbox on the back seat for her to use in transit. It made such an unsteady platform that, after using it, Buckethead would lie on her side for the essential cat habit of scratching at the sand to cover it up.

This is, I have heard, an ancient feline instinct based on making it more difficult for other predators to get on the track of the cat, rather than out of some sense of fastidiousness. Yet this does not explain in any satisfactory way a habit which Geoffrey began in his early maturity and continued all his life.

Dorothy always placed their dishes on waxed paper or aluminium foil. Geoff was forever the glutton, falling upon the food in his own dish and then shouldering Roger away from his dish. Roger always accepted this. Possibly it was a carryover from his maternal interlude. When elbowed aside, he would back off and sit and wait until the other cat was finished. As Geoff had a tendency to eat until everything was gone, Dorothy had to save out Roger's food. Roger never ate much at one time. He liked to leave food and return to it off and on for snacks. Roger has always had a standard routine for showing his distaste for food which does not please him. He stares into the dish, then up at the donor, then into the dish, then up at the donor. He seems to express a bewildered disbelief. Do you *actually* expect me to eat *that?* Why are you doing this to me?

But Geoff's critique was brutally direct. He would plod to his dish. He would lean and snuff and perhaps try one bite. Then, if we were out of the room, we would hear the sounds of his nails against the paper or foil. Scratch, scratch, scratch. Working his way around the dish he would perform a symbolic ritual of covering it up, then plod frowningly away. I can think of no more vivid way he could have expressed his opinion of what had been served him. What particularly infuriated Dorothy was that it might be something he had been eating with gusto for weeks. Cooked hamburg perhaps. Suddenly he would decide there had been quite enough of that. The healthy, well-fed cat will demand changes of diet at almost predictable intervals. It may have something to do with the digestive process. When the demanded change is not forthcoming, he will simply stop eating, despite all appearances of ravenous hunger. The better boarding kennels recognize this cat trait and cater to it when the boarding period is long, even though they continue to give their dogs standardized fare.

We hauled them squalling to Piseco and released them

into an out-of-doors unlike anything they had seen. Here were steep slopes, the black silences of thick woods of pine, hemlock, birch, maple, a thousand hiding places, the strange scents of indigenous animals much larger than mice and moles, curious noises in the night, a lake shore, boats, live fish. They explored with great, quivering caution. We did worry about them up there, then, and in all the years to follow. House cats disappear in Adirondack country, taken by fishers, foxes, wildcats, coydogs and perhaps, sometimes, raccoons, weasels, and those bored, bourboned sportsmen with their mail-order artillery who come racketing in upon us each autumn in search of a dubious manhood.

Once adjusted, the cats relished every minute of it. They would come exhausted back to camp for a quick meal and a short nap, and head on out again. This was a real jungle, man. This was what the cat business was really about. Red squirrels and gray squirrels cursed them. Geoff caught chipmunks, and all but one or two managed their escape. Roger bore proudly back to the porch a shrew the size of an infant's thumb. It had bitten him severely about the chin.

A word here about a strange talent chipmunks have. Johnny discovered it years later when he and his wife were living on a farm in Michigan. Their cats, Jaymie and Grey, caught many chipmunks. They would apparently maim them cruelly, inflicting some sort of injury to the spine. The chipmunks would writhe about, rolling and thrashing once the cat put them down, rolling right toward the cat, a reaction the cats found objectionable. Johnny shot four of the pathetic things to put them out of their misery, and, one day, when he was about to shoot the fifth, it suddenly seemed remarkable that all five could have been injured in exactly the same way, and reacted in the same way.

So he watched. When the chipmunk would roll toward the cat, the cat would back away with a pained expression. The cat would watch it thrash aimlessly in the grass and, confident that it was unable to flee, the cat's attention would wander. The chipmunk writhed ever closer to a

56

thicket and then suddenly shot off into cover, a little streak of pale brown a good safe distance ahead of the cat's belated pounce. Johnny told me that he then realized, to his dismay, he had slain four skilled thespians right in the midst of their art.

We found this hard to believe. When Johnny and Anne brought Grey to Piseco, they called me from the typewriter one afternoon when Grey had caught a chipmunk. The chipmunk lay rigid and unmoving in the cat's jaws. When Grey put it down, that little animal put on the most convincing act I have ever seen. It looked like the final agony, the last wild spasms. It imitated a broken back, and rolled wildly right into the cat. The cat backed away. The chipmunk rolled in random directions, flopping about, then abruptly it sped off to safety. This is apparently a talent shared by chipmunks everywhere and one of the strangest and most specialized defensive instincts I have ever seen. Many animals and even some insects will play dead. But as far as I have been able to tell, only chipmunks play dying.

The lake intrigued Geoffrey far more than it did Roger. The front porch of the hillside camp overlooked the boat dock and the tethered boats. One late afternoon several of us, sitting on the porch, saw Geoff jump down into a skiff. He explored it carefully, sniffing at elderly traces of fish, working his way to the stern. He got up onto the rear seat and from there onto the housing of the outboard motor. The motor was tipped up. Stepping quite daintily, he went cautiously out onto the narrower housing which encloses the drive shaft. When he took a step halfway to the propeller, his weight tilted it down abruptly, dumping him into the lake. Shocked, and doubtlessly furious, he cat-paddled to shore. A soaked cat is a sorry, spavined sight. He moved off into heavy brush, and when we saw him next he was totally dry, fluffy, unconcerned—and probably would have told us that we were all mistaken—it had been some other cat.

When we went out in a boat he would sit on the dock and look after us so wistfully that one day Dorothy took him into a boat and rowed him down to Big Sand. It terrified him. He wanted to jump out but could not quite bring himself to do so. Dorothy let him out at Big Sand so upset he threw up, and she rowed slowly back, with Geoff following along the rocky shore line, making pitiful noises. Perhaps he noticed on that return trip that the shore line was where you go to look for frogs. Years later he owned one.

When our time was up and the next contingent due, we drove back to Clinton. The cats made loud objection the entire way, and I know it was only my imagination, but I seemed to detect in their mournful cries not only their objection to automobiles but also despair that they should be yanked out of paradise with so many woodsy tasks yet undone.

It was at Wanahoo that they became sophisticated and deft about trees. As we sat on the porch we would hear thrashings in the leaves of the smaller trees on the slope of the bank, and then, at our level, a cat face would appear to stare at us. This was a look-at-me, look-at-me device, typical of all young males. Roger made up in reckless abandon what he lacked in co-ordination and judgment. Ascending he was superb, but descending was a frantic and perilous procedure, usually ending with a quick twist, a shower of shredded bark and too long a drop to the ground. Geoff descended with all the careful assurance of a middle-aged lineman. He backed down tree trunks, setting each foothold firmly, looking down over his shoulder exactly as in those pictures of koala bears Down Under. His final drop was usually of one foot or less, followed by a glance up at where he had been.

Also it was at Piseco that they became acquainted with the half brother, Heathcliffe. Geoff and Heath soon learned to tolerate each other, though in grudging fashion. Geoff was not belligerent, at least not when he seemed to feel it a waste of time. He was ready to make those small, constructive adjustments which simplified life. But Rog and Heath reacted to each other with an undying malevolence, noisy warnings, frequent displays of claw and fang, springing back with steam-valve hissings when they met unexpectedly in doorways. It was hate at first sight, and it never lessened.

The world of the cats was growing more complex, and they were learning.

FIVE

It is difficult to appraise the intelligence of any creature, including man. I.Q. in man, maze skills in rats, chickens who play baseball, chimps who pile the boxes to reach a banana, the quicker learning and longer retention of cattle as compared to horses, the circus dog who will walk grotesquely on his front feet—all these things are small illuminations in a great darkness. Too often we confuse some adaptive instinct with reasoning power. There is, for example, one small and enchanting crab in tropical waters which carefully plucks bits of marine weed and, with all the care of a woman doing her own hair, plants these living bits atop his shell so as to make himself less noticeable in his environment. The hermit crab, growing too large for his mobile home shell, will crawl from empty shell to empty shell, using his claws to measure the opening, as businesslike and thoughtful as any carpenter measuring for a shelf. Finding one a suitable degree larger, he will take a long and careful look around before, with frantic haste, he hoists his soft nether portions out of the old home and slips them into the new. (If watching this sort of thing entertains you, grab a hermit crab and put him in a shallow pan of sea water along with several empty shells. Then take one of those tap-icers and carefully crack the back end of the shell he lives in, carefully enough not to damage him. Put him back and watch him pick a new house.)

Another area of confusion in measuring intelligence in animals is our tendency to give the higher marks to the animals most willing to follow orders. (The kid who strains to do well on the I.Q. test may be of lower intelligence than the boy who, lacking sufficient motivation, drifts through it thinking of more entertaining things and makes a lower score.)

Cats are not interested in pleasing anyone by a display of obedience. They are unfailingly pragmatic, which in itself seems to denote a kind of intelligence we are not yet equipped to measure. If a cat can detect no self-advantage in what it is being told to do, it says the hell with it, and, if pressure is brought to bear, it will grow increasingly surly and irritable to the point where it is hopeless to continue. Yet, where the advantage to be gained is clearly related to the task required, the learning process is so acute as to be almost instantaneous. Once learned the feat will be repeated only when the cat is interested in the result.

Geoff was constructed in such a curiously square fashion, we could not help but notice that he had a strange habit, when sitting, of sometimes lifting his forepaws off the floor, sitting much in the manner of a ground squirrel. Sometimes he would adopt this posture for the business of face washing. When he was interested in what people were eating, he would sit near the table, and it took just a little upward gesture of the hand with a morsel in it to bring him up into his sitting position. The implied guarantee of receiving the scrap would keep him there, like a small dog.

Yet after the novelty of that wore off, we did not continue it. It was a question, I suppose, of appearances and of dignity. The cat who emulates, a small, supplicant dog has somewhat the same inadvertent ludicrousness of, for example, a small and extremely fat man. The grin of conviviality is always a little abashed. In some obscure way it shamed the three of us to shame him in a way he accepted so solemnly, and without ever having to discuss it, we all gave it up.

It was Geoffrey, when we lived on College Hill, who provided us with the most memorable example of reasoning power we can remember.

It came about this way. We used to go quite often to the Fort Schuyler Club in Utica with my parents. Johnny was popular with the staff, and they would take him out into the kitchen. One of the other guests had brought in pheasant that fall, and it was being prepared for his table when Johnny went out there. One of the chefs gave him a handful of the big tail feathers of the cock pheasants. He brought them home, and the cats were delighted with them. They could be batted about, knocked into the air, chased, clawed, bitten. They were symbolic birds. In a week or so there were only a few not completely destroyed, and these had been denuded of feathers all except that tuft at the very end which has "eye" markings much like peacock feathers. They were twelve inches of heavy, naked quill with the end tuft.

I should mention here that whereas Roger seemed to prefer co-operative play, either with brother cat or one of the people, Geoff often played alone for long periods, playing solemn and wide-ranging games of solitary field hockey, dribbling a half-bashed ping-pong ball from room to room.

We had finished dinner. Johnny had gone to bed. Roger was sacked out. Dorothy was doing something in the kitchen. I was reading in the living room. She came in and in a hushed voice asked me to come and see what Geoffrey was doing. I went with her and stood quietly in the kitchen doorway and watched him. It was a very long and narrow kitchen. Geoff had invented a game with one of the remaining pheasant feathers. He would circle it and then carefully pick up the quill end in his teeth, adjusting it so that it stuck straight out in front of him. He would flatten himself into the position of the stalk, and then, ears flattened, tail twitching, he would stalk the tuft end of the feather down the length of the kitchen. When he stopped, it would stop. When he moved, it would move. Six feet from the end of the kitchen he would release it, pounce upon it, slide and roll and thump into the wall at the end, biting and kicking hell out of it. Then he would get up, walk slowly around it, studying it, and pick it up again by the quill end and repeat the same performance. I kept count. I watched him do it seven times, and at the end he left it there and walked out of the kitchen. We could never entice him into doing it again. We wanted witnesses. When we told about it, people looked at us with that tolerant skepticism which is so infuriating. They seemed to think we *thought* we had seen Geoff do that. He would never do it again because I imagine he felt he had exhausted the possibilities of that game.

A year or so ago I read a newspaper account of a game invented by some bottlenose dolphins in one of the Florida aquariums. Scientists have recently become very much intrigued by the physiological complexity of the brain of the porpoise, their learning speed, their intricate sounds of communication, even their sense of fun. Several years ago a porpoise inhabiting the outdoor tank at Marineland near Daytona invented a way to amuse himself. A brown pelican was in the habit of filling his belly, then drifting and drowsing in the tank. When he seemed the most off guard, the porpoise would come slowly up under him from behind, then make an explosive underwater turn and, with an upward sweep of his powerful tail, propel the pelican a good twenty feet straight up into the air, flapping and gasping.

But not long ago, in solemn tones, the professors announced they had seen the porpoises at play in a game of their own invention. They had a white sea-bird feather. They would grab it in the lips, take it over to the place where water was constantly pumped into the big tank at high velocity. They would release it in the stream, then chase it and catch it. The professors said this was a reasoned use of a tool, a perfect example of a creative intelligence unsurpassed among all mammals lesser than man, not only because it was of their own devising, but because it was purely for the sport of it, unlike the simian use of objects to knock down food or pelt their enemies.

I like to imagine that those porpoises keep right on playing their feather game. Geoffrey outgrew it after one lengthy session.

Roger, that fall, managed to do something distantly related to the pelican-tossing bit. A woman visited us. She was very afraid of cats. We respect this aberration, and are quite willing to imprison the cats for the duration of such visits. But this woman, being excessively polite, asked us please not to go to such trouble. Geoffrey went off somewhere, but Roger took a great interest in the woman. Roger was always more interested in visitors. He sought all sources of potential amusement. In this case he kept slowly circling the room, staying close to the baseboard, eyeing the woman. It made her nervous enough to frequently lose touch with the conversation. She was in a wing chair.

Finally Roger stopped in the corner behind her. For the poor woman, this was worse than being able to see him pacing and staring at her. She began, trying not to be conspicuous about it, to lean to one side and then the other, casting quick glances around the back of the chair, trying to see where he was. The back of the chair was not high. I estimate it came to about the level of her eyes as she sat there erect, increasingly nervous.

At last she turned all the way around to try to look over the back of the chair. I guess Roger could see her head. At any rate he chose that moment to leap straight up into the air. He did not try to jump onto the back of the chair. He just went up and, with the *ballon,* the levitation of the great male dancers of classic ballet, seemed to stay suspended in the air, a monstrous fright-cat, a foot from the woman's face. We never saw him do that again. He was grabbed and hustled away and shut in a room. But that woman was through. She was close to hysteria. She was pallid and sweaty. Controlling herself with visible effort she left, never to return. The fiend-cat had detected her cowardly heart. When she was gone and we let him out, he went immediately to the living room to look for her. He jumped into the chair, snuffled about, and then sat and began to wash. If a cat can smirk, Roger smirked.

I suspect that this identification by cats of this common

phobia is not as mysterious as legend insists. Fear has an odor. Their noses are keen. Fear is the smell of the victim. And here, intriguingly, is something afraid which is far too big to kill and eat. But there could be sport involved if it could only be induced to run. I think that was what Roger was attempting, to startle the scared thing into flight. What a picture it would have made, that lovely chase around and around the house and over into the tall grass of Saunders' Strip.

That fall we had the incident of the Great Bloat. The cats were full-grown. They were neither nocturnal nor diurnal but trying to get the best of both worlds.

One morning we got up to find Roger visibly distended and in deep sleep. He looked so odd we woke him up. He did not seem ill. He awoke reluctantly, stretched, yawned, and went back to sleep. He slept all that day. Sometimes he would arise with ponderous effort, go drink some water, go outside for a few minutes, come back in, and collapse again. Geoff was entirely normal. We wondered about taking Rog to the vet. Yet he did not feel overly hot. He would not eat, yet he would purr readily when awakened. His coat looked fine. The gloss disappears almost immediately when a cat is not well. We were puzzled. As far as we could tell he slept all that night, and the next day was a repetition of the first, though he did not seem as swollen.

Sam and his boys had been hunting rabbits west of Albany earlier and had discovered that the rabbit feet, properly dried, made cat toys which were used with great enthusiasm. They had sent us four for our cats, and the reception lived up to the advance billing. By the time of the Bloat, two of them had suffered such hard wear Dorothy had thrown them out. The other two, hard as little lengths of fur-covered wood, were in kitchen corners where the cats had batted them.

On the second day of the Bloat I wandered into the kitchen from my office late in the day to make a drink. Geoff was there, so I bent over and picked up a rabbit foot to throw it to him. To my queasy astonishment, it was

66

soft. For a moment I thought one of the dried ones had unaccountably softened. Then I saw that the fur was a paler tan, and that the severed place was ragged and stained dark with dried blood.

Mystery solved. Bloated Cat was showing the visible effects of his one single-minded attempt at gluttony. From the size of the foot we estimated the rabbit had been about half his size, and from the look of the cat he hadn't shared any of it. There is the possibility he caught it. This might account for the heroic attempt to eat it all. We searched and could find no other remnants of rabbit. It was curiously eerie that the foot should be left in the kitchen where the other two were. One could not say whether it was accident or design.

He was a mighty somnolent cat for yet another night, another day, and another night. And then he was a lethargic cat for several days after he had returned to normal size and had begun, sparingly, to eat. We read into his subsequent manner an increase in assurance and perhaps a smiling tendency to reminisce.

Rita became mortally ill that winter. We set up a hospital bed in the living room, and for long, exhausting weeks Dorothy nursed her, administering shots every four hours day and night.

On the day she died, after her body had been taken away, we took a long, aimless drive through that rolling country and knew it was time to get out—not only because Dorothy so badly needed a change of scene, but also because it had been a bad choice of environment for us. We had found there many good and pleasant people, but instead of the intellectual stimulation we had anticipated from a college community, we had found a carefully established pecking order, with status often achieved and maintained through the elegancies of entertaining rather than any quality of wit or insight. As far as other outsiders resident down in the village were concerned, Dorothy treasures a ghoulish memory of a Save The Children meeting she attended whereat it was decided that those village women who wanted to work at this charity but were not quite socially acceptable could be put in some sort of affiliated setup whereby they could work but would not be entitled to attend the teas. She attended no further meetings. We also discovered that we were the unwelcome targets of an avid and undisciplined curiosity. It is a mistake, unless you have an actor's flair and a poseur's inclinations, to be The Writer in a small community. No matter how limpid your normal behavior, how rotarian your tastes and habits, your every move will be examined and so interpreted that it fits the myths the townspeople choose to believe.

For example, not long ago four of us in the writing profession sat at lunch of a Friday in the Plaza Restaurant in Sarasota and figured that between us we represented 129 years of marriage, each of us to but one spouse, and had Joe Hayes and Wyatt Blassingame been there, also writers who reside in the area and often come to Friday lunch, we could have added another hunk of years under the same stipulation, fifty or more. And not an alcoholic or an addict in the lot. The same kind of statistic would apply to the better-known professional painters who live there.

There are so many writers and painters along the west coast of Florida, the community considers us as normal as if we were real estate brokers or insurance agents.

It makes for a restful environment, but in all the less sophisticated communities of America the mythology will not countenance such dullness. They want the heady moral indulgence of finding something which they can disapprove.

Also, though we were managing to stay even, we were not able to accumulate any reserve. Mexico seemed a good answer. Unless we could save something, we could not start the camp at Piseco.

We rented the College Hill house to a pleasant couple who asked for and received permission to pursue their pigeon-keeping hobby in one of the three garages, and for a ridiculously small rent discount for food, they agreed to harbor our cats.

The three of us set off towing the same cargo trailer, this time behind a newer black Ford convertible, learning Spanish words all the way down by means of flash cards.

Our destination, Cuernavaca, was made inevitable by our both getting hooked on that superb novel *Under the Volcano* by Malcolm Lowry. It was 1948.

That previous winter was the only time we saw our cats exposed to snow, and indeed the last time they had a snowy out-of-doors to cope with.

Their reactions to dirty weather were quite different. Roger despised snow. He hated to put his feet into it. He acted as though he were being forced to walk upon some incredible nastiness. Yet he has never minded light rain. He goes out into it, drinks out of puddles, comes in matted and happy.

Geoffrey hated rain in any degree, and at Clinton he developed his rain procedure. Going to his window and finding it spattering off his cat shelf into his face, he would back away and go to a closed door and start hollering. The door had to be opened so he could look out and see that it was raining out there too. He would go to the next door and repeat the request. That house had many doors. Satisfied it was raining everywhere, he would either stay in or, under physiological compulsion, brace himself, go out his window, and race for shelter.

We both remember the time much later in Florida when, after we had told him for years that he was an idiot, he proved his point. The summer rains in Florida are often so brief and so concentrated, it can be raining on one side of the street and quite dry on the other. One day at Point Crisp, Geoff started that door-to-door nonsense, backing away from the heavy rain each time. He hollered at the back door, and Dorothy opened it for him, and it was dry and bright out there. He plodded on out with that matter-of-factness which seemed to say that he had always known it would work one day.

But snow did not bother him as it did Roger. When it was quite deep he would bound through it with as much aplomb as any rabbit, in fact leaving tracks which resembled rabbit tracks. In his youngest days at State Street he would go out onto that flat part of the roof and sit in the snow.

Seen from the rear while in normal sitting position,

Geoff was a ludicrous sight. The way he sat gave him a perfect pear shape. He was a hairy schmoo, with those tufted ears on top. I treasure one memory of him out on the terrace at College Hill. I happened to glance through the glass doors and saw him out there, sitting with his back toward the doors. He was in about four inches of snow, and he had been there so long his body heat had melted him down into it.

SIX

———◆———

At Cuernavaca we found a small brick house behind a wall. It was at 8 Jacaranda Street, a long block east of the main highway, about five miles north of the city, and with a view of the volcanoes from our small front porch.

We acquired a part-time gardener for the small yard and garden, and a full-time maid named Esperanza. We located a private school for Johnny. Dorothy coped with the public market. Our neighbors on either side were a Mexican dentist and a Mexican colonel. Much later, when I computed our total expenses for the best part of the year we were there, I found that the total for everything—including entertainment, side trips, and typewriter ribbons—averaged out at $115 a month.

There were savage dogs in our neighborhood. One, owned by a mystery woman who lived diagonally across the street and was reputed to be the mistress of some important Mexico City politico, was so damned large and unpleasant that when we ventured outside our gates at night on foot, I carried a rock or a club.

We suspect that this dog inflicted the wound on Pancha, the bleeding, terrorized cat who came scrabbling under our closed gate one day with a deep, fresh wound in her back. We gave her care and refuge, and she responded with warmth and trust. She was a pretty and dainty little cat, and she obviously had no intention of ever going back out where the dogs were. She was so obviously hardly more than a kitten that we could not believe she was pregnant. But with an increasing obviousness, she was, beyond doubt.

As her time grew near and she began a rather absent-minded investigation of dark corners and closets, Dorothy fixed her a box and introduced her to it, and she seemed content with it.

One morning I got up before dawn and drove with a friend down to Lake Tequesquitengo and fished for bass. We came back at noon, and I stopped at his place and had some Oso Negro gin with local ginger ale. John Commerford was a good fishing companion, but he made those drinks heavy.

(John's wife, Pearl, was taking Spanish lessons, but John insisted sign language could get him anything he wanted. He went into town one day to buy a fly swatter and stopped at a likely shop on the narrow street leading to the public market. Making random, fluttering gestures with his left hand, and saying, "Zzzzzzzzz," John held the imaginary swatter in his right hand, then struck, saying "Pow!" After about two solid minutes of this the totally blank expression of the proprietor turned to a beaming grin of comprehension. He ran into his storeroom and returned proudly with a box of ping-pong balls. John joined La Perla for the language lessons.)

I wobbled two blocks home through a garish unreality of daylight, undone by the early hours, the drive, the fishing and the gin. Dorothy had gone marketing. I stretched out on my back on the bed and fell asleep. About an hour later I was awakened by cat claws needling into my side. My right arm was outstretched, and Pancha had nestled into my armpit. She was purring very loudly and became louder when I stroked her. Every so often she would stop purring, dig her claws into me, then begin purring again. It seemed odd behavior. I had my hand on her the next time it happened, and I felt a strange rippling which seemed to start at her shoulders and go down to her back heels. I lifted my head and stared down at her and suddenly realized what was going on. My first impulse was to hustle her to her box, but then I thought that if she had that much trust, if she had selected that particular place to have her kittens, then the least I could do would be go along with it.

By the time I heard Dorothy arrive, we'd had the first kitten. Pancha was very tidy and efficient about it. She had three, and one was dead. Except during the labor pains, she purred every moment. Birthing done, she was content to be moved into the box with her damp, blind family. The kittens were a male and a female, and we named them Brujo and Bruja—he-witch and she-witch.

By then we had become friendly with Van and Scottie MacNair, who lived one diagonal long block away in a little house called La Casita, just off the main highway. Their boys, younger than Johnny, were in the same school. Van was also free-lancing in magazine fiction. We became close, and despite subsequent geographical dislocations, have remained close. Van is now Director of Public Relations for the Los Angeles County Museum.

Their boys wanted a cat, and in due time we gave them Brujo. Van had a studied and skeptical indifference to the whole idea, an attitude which reminded me strongly of my own back on State Street.

It was not long before Scottie reported that Brujo had become Van's cat, accustomed to staying with Van in the room where he worked and watching him companionably from the couch. Van maintained his amused tolerance for a respectable amount of time, and then at last admitted that it was one hell of a fine cat, and he had never known a cat intimately before, and they were splendid animals indeed.

One evening after Brujo was almost full-grown, Van came wandering dejectedly over in the early evening to tell us that Brujo had been missing and they had all gone calling for him, hunting for him, searching the highway ditches and the fields, and had at last found him fifty yards or so behind the house, torn to pieces by dogs. The whole MacNair family was crushed.

Bruja fared better. We found her a home with an acquaintance, a lady who lived alone in a large house with swimming pool and staff of servants. We learned later that Bruja was living on tinned chicken breast and cream and wore a little collar with her name on it.

We received a letter from our tenants saying they had found a house they wanted to buy. They gave us notice and asked what they should do with the cats. We wrote them to take them to Dr. Sellman in Utica, and we wrote him to expect them. That was in the spring of 1949.

In the summer we gave Pancha to the MacNairs and headed home. Later we heard that Pancha's fertility served to quench Van's new enthusiasm for cats and, indeed, even made Scottie look slightly grim. In a very short time La Casita was bulging with cats, Pancha producing them faster than the MacNairs could place them.

We stayed at the Clinton house just long enough to sort all our possessions, dispose of a lot of items, and put the rest in storage. Whenever we started to fill an empty box, we would find Geoffrey in it. The cats showed no effects from being deserted so long. They did a lot of looking for a dog who no longer lived there. Johnny toted Geoff around by the hour during the first days of reunion.

There was one change in Roger which requires explanation. As a very young cat he had picked up a strange habit. He would bite. But certainly not out of malice or bad temper. I believe it was originally related to his habit of washing brother cat and, in the midst of that ceremony, taking a tentative nip. Roger's bite was an expression of pleasure and affection. Dorothy has always gotten the worst of it, as she is barelegged more often than I am. Roger would wind around your ankles, purring, nudging his head against you, and all of a sudden he would bite. Riding your shoulder he would take a nip at the side of your face. He bit legs because they were handiest. He would not bite through cloth. He had to have a little bare skin handy. We were members of his community, and by God, anybody was entitled to bite anybody in that same spirit of affectionate fun. The difficulty was that Roger would bite anybody, anyone, that is, who was in his house. If they were there it meant we all accepted him or her, and they were biteable.

I contributed to this strange social habit by, when Roger was purring and nudging me, hoisting a pant leg to give him a target area. We remember the time a young doctor paid a house call on State Street to look at Johnny. Roger rubbed against his leg and was ignored. Then, standing with his front feet to one side of the doctor's shoe and his hind feet over on the other side, he curled his neck around, gently hoisted the doctor's pant cuff with his muzzle, and bit him just above his short sock.

In chopping at people's knees with his little red rubber hammer, the doctor never achieved a reflex action as good as the one Roger gave him. Roger sailed all the way across the room. We tried to explain. The doctor said it was perfectly all right, hadn't broken the skin. But he kept a wary eye on the cat the rest of the time he was there.

We believe that as he grew older, Roger developed into a connoisseur of the reactions of strangers to an unexpected cat bite. He stopped giving the advance warning of the nudging and leg-twining and began to favor the back of the leg a few inches above the ankle. A sudden leap, a hearty yelp, a spin, and stare of disbelief seemed the most satisfying.

When we brought the cats home from Dr. Sellman's we discovered that Roger still bit. However, the procedure was changed. Whereas before he would bite and then stand in calm friendly appraisal, now he would bite, leap three feet away, bend all his four knees, lay his ears back, and obviously wait for the expected whack. Evidently our tenants had thought they could cure him by returning a whack for every bite. But Roger had driven his own bargain. Bite away, and endure the whack, and bite again another day.

Though over the years this conditioned reflex has almost disappeared, there is still a slight suggestion of it left.

After the bite there is the slightest crouch, a faint flattening of the ears, a moment of watchful waiting for what might come next.

Also, after almost a year, he remembered the sock game. This originally came under the heading of tormenting the cat. Some mornings he would be so interested in giving me a friendly nip as I was getting up, before I could get my trousers on, that in self-defense I quickly shoved a sock over his head. In horror he tried to back out of the darkness, the foot part dangling and swinging like the misshapen trunk of some strange little hairy elephant. He backed into a corner and then clawed the sock off, gave me that cat look, and walked out of the bedroom.

On subsequent mornings I did the same thing. It depressed him less each time, though he continued to make a great effort to avoid it. In time he learned that he could see through the weave of the sock, and then he became intrigued. He would walk around, looking through the sock, and when he tired of it, he had only to step on the foot end and pull his head free. Thus it became ritual, and when I picked up a sock he would stand still and wait for me to put it on his fool head.

He remembered this game and still does, though now it is a very seldom thing. He is rarely up before we are, and when there is a chance for the sock game it is a kind of ancient reassurance, though as he stands wearing it, purring audibly, I wonder just who is humoring whom. These days I pull the sock off, and that is the only variation.

That summer of 1949 we took our short turn at Wanahoo. Dorothy had drawn the plans for the house. We went over them with Floyd Abrams, the local builder, and told him to get started whenever he could. We boarded the cats with Dr. Sellman and told him that when we had found a place to spend the school year, we would send him word to send the cats to us by Railway Express.

Once again we set out for New Mexico. We decided to follow the coast and dip down into Florida and back out again. We crossed over through Orlando and through Tampa, and on a bright, hot September day came across the Courtney Campbell Causeway and into Clearwater.

What's so wrong with this? we asked each other.

By the next day we had located and rented a little frame house on Acacia Street on Clearwater Beach, two blocks from the Gulf, owned by a friendly and generous lady named Mrs. Payne. By the following day we were reasonably well settled in, and Johnny had started school. We sent for the cats. On the third day an officer of the law arrived with a warrant for a traffic violation. Under nature of violation was written: Child in school. You have to wear Florida plates to enjoy that privilege.

We wondered how the cats would weather the trip down and how they would adjust to the semi-tropics.

SEVEN

———◆———

Though it was certainly not long ago, shipping pets by Railway Express was a far more plausible venture in the late forties and first half of the fifties than it is today. The cost of shipping two big cats in a big plywood crate with wire windows at either end was not exorbitant. You would cover the box floor with torn paper, fasten their water dishes and food dishes solidly into the corners, tack a sack of canned food with can opener to the outside, and glue simple feeding instructions to the outside. Railway Express would fasten a card to the crate upon which employees en route would write the day and time they were fed and watered, and sign their names.

The cats would ride from Utica to Florida and back in an average two and a half days and arrive in a state so mildly traumatic that a couple of hours would see them back to normal.

But each year the rates went up, and each year the train schedules worsened, and each year the men along the way seemed to give less of a damn about a pair of damn cats, and they arrived in increasingly worse condition until, finally, it became impossible.

So this, too, relates to the myth of our ever increasing standard of living. We live in a culture where service is increasingly slovenly, surly, and reluctant, where schedules mean less and less, where every species of life including the human animal is held in less esteem each year, where all the glossy gadgetry disintegrates at an ever increasing rate, where mediocrity in all things has become a goal—with all excellence suspect.

There is nothing mysterious, of course, about this accelerated decline. My sixth-grade geography teacher told us that the individual life was cheap and cruelly used in China because of the terrible population density of four hundred millions of them. Today we approach half that number in less than half the space, so that the mass insularity of the anthill is the inevitable result. Thirty-seven witnesses can watch a woman murdered. Millions of kids can learn group adjustment as if it were a commendable skill. Over half the humans in the world have no memory of World War II. In an acceleration of the technologies, it is cheaper to repeat experimentations than to conduct a search for previous results. As life gets ever more inconvenient, trashified, and irritating, it is possible to convince through electronic repetition the brand-new millions that everything is, in fact, getting better and better and better.

It is still possible to ship pets. One purchases an approved crate constructed of light metal. One drives the necessary distance to a major airport where there will be a direct flight to the major airport nearest the destination. One makes the air-express arrangements, confirms the loading, then phones someone at the far end to go to the airport and arrange to receive the animals. It is wise to get the proper tranquilizers from the vet so the animals' response to extreme trauma will be dulled. And be prepared for heavy expense. This is yet another one of the conveniences of the jet age.

A pleasant voice over the telephone told us that a box of cats had arrived, and we drove at once to the Railway

Express office in Clearwater, put the car top down, and loaded the rather fetid crate into the back seat. It mewed in a dreary way. Back at Acacia Street we set it down in the driveway, and I undid the hasp and opened it, and the cats arched out, blinking at the bright sun. Their first response, then and thereafter, was to find a place of dust or powdered marl and roll and roll. Then, as always, exploration was carried on in shoulder to shoulder formation. Always, after they had been in a crate together, or after they had been at a boarding kennel in the same cage, they tended to stay very close together for a period which related directly to the length of time they had shared confinement. It seemed to represent both habit and security.

And both of them would holler. They would walk around and, at intervals of two or three minutes give a yowling and forlorn cry. We were never able to figure out why they did this. It is possible that when a wild feline moves to a new part of the forest, instinct requires this announcement of the new address, but one would think it might make prospective meals harder to catch.

We recall one time, one of the last times we had them shipped down by rail, after service had deteriorated badly. It had taken four days. One or both of them had been sick and had diarrhea. Their crate was horrid. I opened it in the driveway of our Point Crisp house. Geoff hopped out and with his lumpy, purposeful stride walked directly to our thick hedge of Australian pine, stuck his head into it, and just stood there for a long long time.

After their tandem tour of the premises in Clearwater we introduced them to their kitchen corner where their first Florida snack was served, and then to their window. After much washing, hollering, investigating, they settled down to the long naps of tired tourists, sleeping so close they were in familiar contact.

There was record heat that fall in Clearwater. The cats searched for relatively cool corners. At times they panted audibly like dogs, pink tongues lolling. They ate lightly, drank often, and except in the cool of early morning, made no unnecessary movements. The big tree outside our bedroom windows was full of noisy birds.

We noticed that Geoff wasn't doing very well. He became very unresponsive. He ate less and less. His chunky sides sagged until his backbone began to look scrawny and pathetic, and at times there would be a milky film over his eyes.

A veterinary with an establishment near the St. Pete dog track was recommended to us, and we took Geoffrey there. The pleasant man examined him and asked us questions about him.

At last he gave his surprising diagnosis. Geoffrey was psychologically depressed. When cats become depressed they show what is called the third eyelid, a milky membrane that comes up from under the lower lid. He just simply did not care for Florida. He was homesick for a terrain he had found more agreeable. Recommendation: Give him a great deal of attention, coddling, affection. Try to keep him entertained. We had been respecting what we thought was ill health by trying not to bother him too much, and this apparently was further contributing to his state of depression. It further confirmed our own estimate of the complexity of these furry house guests to have what was apparently an eminently practical and businesslike D.V.M. tell us that cats in this condition will actually sometimes become weaker and more withdrawn and eventually die.

Old Turtle-head got unexpected benefit from Geoff's therapy. There had always been a perceptible jealousy. From the beginning, if we paid too much exclusive attention to Roger, Geoff would trudge gloomily away. If we paid too much attention to Geoff, Roger—in exasperation—would bite him. So we all had the habit, if we patted one cat in passing, we patted the other if he was nearby.

Geoff endured the attentions for a time and then gradually became more responsive. He began to eat better. The third eyelid was seen less frequently and then not at all. He filled out again, and that lumpy pacer's stride took on the purposeful porkiness of old. He found a good hunting area in an overgrown vacant lot nearby. He brought in a huge, indignant bluejay who, when released, spent a good part of the afternoon on a low limb screaming obscenities and evidently accusing Geoff of unfair tactics. Both cats filled the house with lizards. That was something Roger could catch, too, though not in the quantity Geoffrey achieved. Roger could never quite comprehend the standard tactic of the small green ones. When they would try to scurry away he would plant a foot on their tail. The lizard would keep on going and the little green tail would writhe for a little time and then grow still. He would stare at the tail, snuff at it, look at the lizard's escape route, then cock his head to one side and then the other. Cats and dogs express bewildered curiosity in exactly the same manner.

We learned that the housebound lizards could easily be induced to run into the open mouth of a brown paper bag after the cats had lost interest. We did miss some of the little green ones, and later we would find their bodies clinging to window screens in the high corners between screen and sash. Totally dried and darkened, they looked far more prehistoric, savage little symbols of the frightful giants of the quaking earth an aeon ago. Johnny began saving the perfect ones, along with fishbones and bird skulls and the empty hulls of giant insects, shark teeth, oddly shaped stones. When, not too many years later, he began to draw with serious intent, began to show that almost ruthless unconcern toward other activities which is the plight and the strength of the artist, he turned to these things as models as he trained eye and hand.

The cats brought in another kind of lizard, which none of us cared for and which even the cats seemed reluctant to fool with once they released them in the house. These were larger ones, fat, thick, black, damp, and short-legged. Their escape efforts on hardwood or linoleum were more snakelike than lizardlike, and when Geoff brought one in he would have his lips pulled high in his gesture of distaste.

Having heard that some of the small Florida lizards were poisonous, having been told horrific tales of crazed and paralyzed cats, we were worried about what might happen. But they certainly had no inclination to eat the lizards. Roger, for several days, had a swelling and infection which could have come from a lizard bite, but we could not be certain that was the cause.

At Piseco and at College Hill we had learned that our cats loved to accompany us on walks. Geoff was happy to plod along at our speed, staying several steps behind us like a small dog, pausing sometimes to investigate some interesting scent along the way, then hurrying to catch up to his self-assigned position. Roger made a vast, nutty game out of it, hiding until we had passed, then rocketing by us and hiding again to either pounce out as we passed, or to repeat the previous performance. If walks became too long it was usually Roger who would lose interest first and go on about his own affairs.

At Acacia Street this habit became a nuisance. After Geoff had recovered his morale, Dorothy and I fell into the habit of, after dinner, walking through the pleasant night to a little bar several blocks south and over on the other side of Mandalay Road, the main street on Clearwater Beach. The cats thought this was a splendid ceremony and tried to go along with us. But there was too good a chance of their getting run over on Mandalay either going over there with us or wandering around the area after we had gone inside. So we would close the cat window if they were in the house. If they weren't, we would walk and keep an eye out for them and then con them into coming close enough for capture so we could take them home and shut them in.

But you cannot safely con a cat very many times. They arrived at a catlike solution. When we were ready to leave for our pair of cold beers and game of table shuffleboard, the cats would be outside. Calling them was useless. They were invisible. So we would start out and look back and see the pair of them, night after night, walking together along the sidewalk following us, a half block away. We would see those two conspirators under the street lights, and if we called, they would stay just a half block behind. If we went back, they would melt into the darkness to reappear again, a half block behind us after we gave up the hunt. When we started home, after a half block or a block, both cats would suddenly be underfoot, perfectly willing to be picked up and carried across Mandalay and set down again, and they gamboled and horsed around all the way home.

Roger chilled us to the bone one night on the way home. At a cross street near the house we stopped on the corner to let a slow-moving car go by. Just as it was reaching the corner, Roger pulled his idiot trick of rocketing past us. It was under a street light. He cut it so fine he actually had to add a little extra curve to get around the far front wheel of the car. We yelled at him, I think after he was out of danger, it happened so fast. When we crossed with Geoff, he was waiting over there with that cat grin of high spirits, fun and games, prancings in the night.

In the spring at Acacia Street, mockingbirds nested all over that area. At another time and another place I had acquired considerable respect for one mockingbird talent. We had stopped on a Saturday night at a motel in southern Texas near Harlingen. There was a navigable stream behind it. At dawn Sunday morning some jackass began cutting hardwood boards with a power saw. I complained at the office when we checked out. The man at the desk said it was a mockingbird, who had learned the noise from a small boat yard nearby. I did not really believe it until finally I tracked the sound down and located the creature in a treetop being a power saw.

Just last fall at Point Crisp there was another startling example of the mockingbird art. Roger had a hair ball he had been trying to get rid of for several days. In his attempt to disgorge it, he would crouch and make an unmistakable gasping, wheezing, creaking sound of nausea that would go on and on without satisfactory result. It was a rhythmic, repetitive noise. He didn't seem very well last fall, and the effort would leave the old boy shaky. It was warm and the doors onto the screened terrace were open. I had come downstairs from my office, and as I walked through Dorothy's studio I heard him straining away out on the terrace, so I went out there to check on him. I didn't see him anywhere. I went into the living room and saw him asleep on the couch and thought I had imagined it all. Then, behind me out on the terrace the sound started again. I looked out and saw a large mockingbird sitting on a low limb of a bush just outside the screening and perhaps three feet above ground level, being a sick cat. Roger would often go out there to be sick, and the bird was as close as he could get to the place Rog usually went. As he made the noise he was cocking his head this way and that, peering in through the screen, quite obviously looking for the cat. I called Dorothy, and she listened to him, to the uncanny precision of the imitation, and we decided that the bird was, in what he construed as an accurate manner, calling the cat.

In the warm spring nights on Acacia Street the mockingbirds sang all night long, repeating their improvisations in series of four, adding fragments of cardinal, bluejay, mourning dove, gull, heron, red-winged blackbird. It could get to be compulsive, counting the series of four and listening for an eventual repetition. I managed to teach one of them a wolf whistle and, sooner or later, that would also crop up in that interminable serenade of nesting time.

The cats learned respect for an entirely different attribute of the nesting mockingbird. Jays would make an endless squawking fuss at such piercing volume that often they could drive a cat back indoors by getting on his nerves. Other types of birds would, like the jays, make tentative passes at the cats, staying at a safe distance. But those mockingbirds, during the nesting season, actually pecked hell out of both cats. When either cat crossed an open space by daylight, a mockingbird would take a bomb run from behind the target, come in low and hard and fast, administer one good knock on the skull, and zoom straight back up out of reach. The experience was not only painful, but it was a horrid indignity. Both cats had three and four little peck holes on top of the head centered in little bald, gray, circular patches half-dime size where hair stopped growing. Both of them learned defensive tactics, though it seemed to pain them. In daylight they would walk under the protection of hedges and bushes or walk very close to the side of the house. When one of them came to the end of his protection of the moment, he would stop, select the next shelter, look around with obvious anxiety, then run across the open space. The holes healed, and the hair grew back, and in time they learned how to take advantage of all shelter without looking so nervous about it—in fact, giving the impression the entire procedure was entirely accidental.

There are not as many mockingbirds these days, and with the decrease in numbers their boldness has lessened. Their preferred diet is bulky insects, and their clan has not prospered on the fare of poisoned bugs we have provided for them in our ghastly and futile efforts to eliminate mosquitoes. Mosquitoes, adjusting quickly to poisons, achieving immunity to one dire brew after the next, are bigger, huskier, and more numerous than ever, and now thrive all year round in Florida. For the first time in modern history the spraying equipment in the Fort Myers area was used so intensively all winter that by spring when the millions turned to billions, there had been no chance to dismantle, clean, and maintain their hard-pressed and increasingly futile equipment.

Ten and twelve years ago, both at Piseco Lake and in Florida, in the long dusks of hot weather there were shimmering legions of dragonflies, darting, wheeling, feeding on the mosquito, the gnat, the sand fly—such numbers of them that sometimes they would perceptibly darken the sky. But we poisoned them with the sprays, and they are gone. Now, at Piseco, we get stung all season rather than just up to about the eighth of July on the average, and in Florida we get welted all year round instead of from April to October.

Rachel Carson made a profound objection on the basis we are poisoning all the living things on our planet. I object on the basis we are far worse off now than we were when we started. Ask the ranchers who, in these recent years of incomparable progress have had thousands of head of cattle killed by mosquitoes so dense the young beef have choked to death and the mature animals have, in panic, run themselves to death. I think the mockingbirds would vote for immediate federal control of this stupendous idiocy presently conducted for the most part by self-styled experts who can't even read the warnings on the container. The mosquito-control man in Sarasota County, Mel Williams, is one of those rarities, a valid expert, who feels that spraying is a questionable and partial answer. He gets results by eliminating the breeding areas, but we can do nothing about the clouds of trillions of them which blow in from less enlightened counties when wind and weather are exactly right.

One point has never been properly emphasized in this endemic condition of overspraying by local governmental bodies throughout the country. Capital expenditures are made on a low-bid basis, and under these conditions there is small chance for any squeeze, grease, or rakeoff. But the lethal goo for the spray equipment is purchased as are other "supplies," and here it is tradition in thousands of counties and thousands of communities that the men in office get their little sweetening in the form of kickbacks from the suppliers, thereof be the item paper clips, liquid soap, prison potatoes, or compounds so lethal that children have died after playing with the containers they came in months after they have been emptied. So when Joe Courthouse needs pocket money, he will cheerfully drench his community with another thousand dollars' worth of bird-killer, explaining that he is fighting the good fight against noxious, disease-bearing bugs. If they buy a hundred-year supply of liquid perfumed soap for the city-hall washrooms, they are in trouble. But you never pile up an incriminating stockpile of poison. You can spread it as fast as you can buy it, and so can the man who beats you in the next election. And the more attractive the kickback, the bigger the volume. No wonder it has become such a huge, profitable industry in an astonishingly short time.

Federal licensing of compounds and federal permits for each spray project based on prior saturation of the area would take a lot of the beguiling charm out of this gravy train.

Also, in Florida, it would be very interesting to find some way of hamstringing the arrogant and powerful citrus industry so that the terrifying discovery of four or five Mediterranean fruit flies would not immediately result in the air-dropping of untold tons of poison of unknown side effects on humans, birds, and animals in densely populated areas. Fellows, how come they manage to have so much fruit in the places the fruit fly comes from?

Geoffrey, of the lumpy paws and stumpy walk, was always more Johnny's cat than anyone's. Then became Dorothy's when Johnny went off to school.

Roger the Cat, in a mood benign.

Roger and the lizard Impasse.

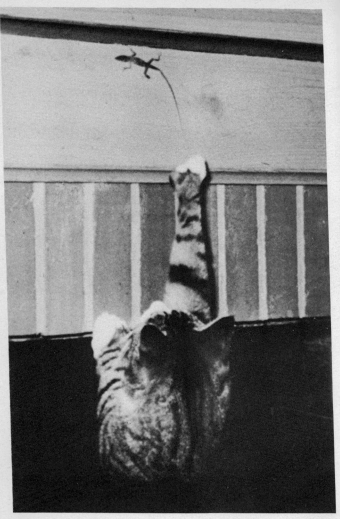

Roger entertains a savage Florida saurian at the Point Crisp house. They almost always got away after a cat brought them in.

Our nephew, John Prentiss, poses with the first big small-mouth bass he ever caught in Piseco Lake. Geoffrey the Cat snuffs, rubs, and purrs with anticipatory appreciation.

After a long day of writing, a pair of happy old cats makes restful company.

Knees in swimming at Piseco Lake with Johnny, our son, and his wife, Anne. She liked to dive and come up behind you and honk very loudly.

Dorothy could never go out on the water bicycle without Knees coming along for the ride, with clarion calls of triumph and pleasure. "Here we come, everybody."

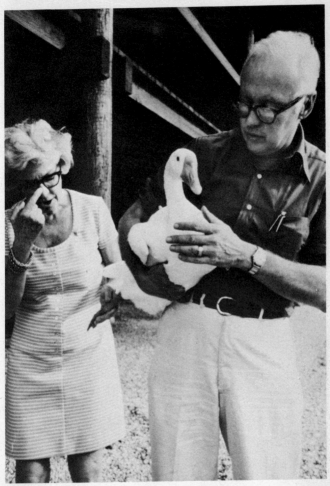

Here Knees is not objecting to being held, but is dubious about having Dorothy examine her foot. She had been limping from an oyster shell cut in the webbing.

Knees expressed pleasure in food with a continual little chuckling, chortling, cooing sound while eating. Watermelon was her favorite, and she would eat it down to green rind no thicker than shoe leather. She is on the rocks in front of the camp at Piseco, with Big Marsh Mountain in the distance.

This is Roger, a little over the hill, getting that slightly hollow-cheeked look of an ancient noble gentleman.

When Dorothy or I picked Knees up, she made a quick token struggle, then became docile and content, and quite curious about what was going to happen next.

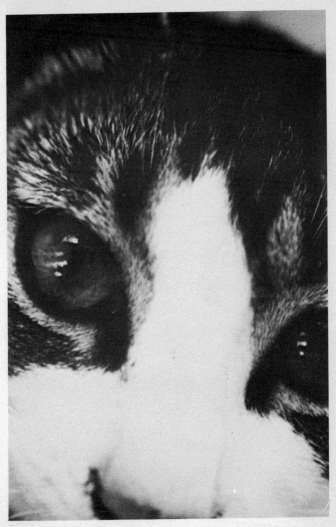

When Johnny and Anne got a cat of their own, his face had markings like Roger's. His name is Frodo.

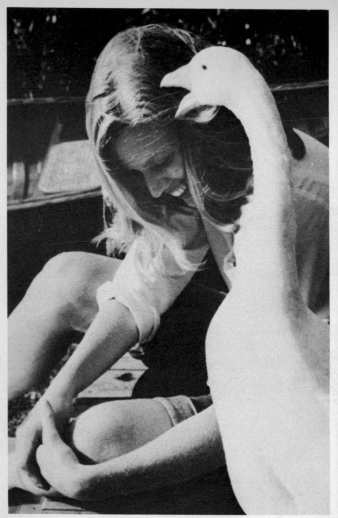

John Prentiss, who caught the bass, also caught and married this strawberry blonde named Kristin. This was the first day Knees saw her. Knees, cooing and chortling with delight, spent the best part of an hour preening and grooming that lovely hair, strand by strand, with infinite care and delicacy, right from the scalp down to the ends.

Knees felt safest on the point of rocks in front of the camp at Piseco Lake.

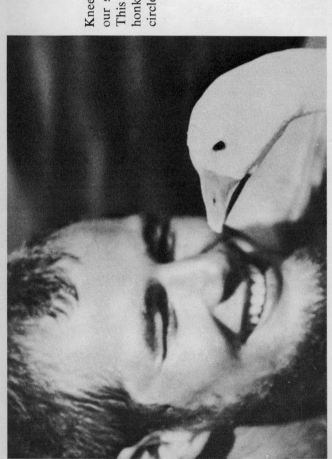

Knees, swimming with our son in Piseco Lake. This required much honking, and many mad circles underwater.

The cats reached another point of evolvement during residence on Acacia Street. Roger perfected his con-artist technique and became a shamelessly lazy slob. In the very beginning he did all the washing of himself and the kitten brother. Somewhere along the line there must have come a time when he did half. But by that winter he arrived at the permanent minimum. After eating they would wash each other's faces. Rather, Rog would give Geoff a couple of apparently diligent licks to get Geoff started. They would sit facing each other. Roger would suffer himself to be thoroughly washed, returning not a lick, fatuously enjoying every moment of it. As soon as Geoff began to show signs of stopping, Rog would give him another couple of swipes, and that would get Geoff going again. Roger, that winter, began to wear the visible signs of the con artist—a shining white face and tattle-tale-gray feet. Cats do not wash each other's feet. Geoff was always tidy. He took care of himself in his spare time.

A cat—fed, clean, content, and pleasantly tired from outdoor adventure—seems to have a curious ability to find some place to rest which will put it on display in a pleasing fashion. It is such a subtle trait it is most difficult to detect. Cats like high places. They like soft places. Often these are also artistically pleasing to the human eye when adorned by resting cat. Except in the very hottest weather, a cat's sleeping and resting positions are graceful. When it is very hot, the trusting cat will sleep on its back, hind legs splayed, front legs sticking up in the air, bent loosely at the wrist. We had an opportunity for many years of observation of these two animals, and we are both convinced that given a choice of two places of equivalent cat comfort, more than 50 per cent of the time the cat will select the one where it looks the best. For example, if there is a dark couch with two dark cushions and one cushion in a bright, clear color, all equally soft, the cat will spend 60 per cent of his couch time on one or another of the dark cushions, and 40 per cent on the bright one, thus showing a preference though not a consistent and invariable one.

Both cats broke things. Roger would bust them in reckless, racing cat-games. Geoff had a far more deliberate procedure. Resting quietly on a mantel, a bureau, a table, a breakfast bar, he would reach out and start gently patting some frangible thing toward the edge, moving it a quarter of an inch per pat. When it fell and shattered, he would hang over the edge and stare down at all the pieces, then stare at whoever was chewing him out with a sort of What-do-you-know-about-that! expression. Sure broke, didn't it?

As the school year drew to a close we realized we could spend our first full summer at Piseco. We had been in correspondence with Floyd Abrams about the camp, and it had been well started, and we could be there for the rest of the work. We made arrangements to rent a small camp not far along the lake shore from Wanahoo, almost directly across the lake from the new camp. We wanted to return to Clearwater, but the house on Acacia Street was too small. Before we left we found a larger house on Bruce Street, several blocks further north along the island, where there would be less traffic than on the Acacia corner, and acquired it long enough before we left so that we could carry things over and store them there, little by little.

A neighbor on Bruce told us during one of these trips that there were cats living under the house, a female and a litter of half-grown kittens too wild and scary to get close to. She said she had been feeding them, but she was going away and did not know how they would manage. She said that there was also a tremendous black tomcat in the area, equally homeless and unapproachable. This is a too-common situation in Florida. Sappy tourists who stay for a few months acquire the pretty kitty for the kids, then deliberately abandon it when they leave rather than take it with them or deliver it to the animal shelter. As a result there are thousands of cats in a semi-wild state, living in uncleared lots and in wild areas of the keys, scavenging for a living and doing badly at it. There is no point in railing at the class of human who will do this. Theirs is an insensate stupidity beyond the possibility of shame or blame. If you, reading this, have a vague uneasy memory of having abandoned a vacation cat somewhere, rest assured that darling kitty did not find a nice home. It ended in the brush, rail-thin, scabrous, and scared, wondering what the hell happened to the darling people. Cats hang around a long, long time before they finally give up. They have a powerful sense of place—a den-affinity. To be locked out of the den is beyond comprehension. It is only the transients like ours who learn to unpack their suitcases anywhere.

We borrowed a cat trap from the humane society, an oblong cage with a trigger-place for the food which would drop the wire gate down. We would set it in the evening and go over and check it in the morning. One at a time we caught the female and her half-grown brood. The terror of the trap loosens the bowels. It was an untidy chore driving them to the shelter, hosing the trap down, resetting it. The animal shelter would try to place them, and, failing that, mete out a swift, painless death.

After we had cleaned out the colony under the house, we kept setting the trap and baiting it. But it remained empty. I caught a glimpse of that tom disappearing into a palmetto patch, looking back over his shoulder at me. The sun caught the high gloss of his black coat. He did not slink or cringe. He prowled, obviously foraging successfully, too savvy for box traps. Soon it was time to go, and we gave up the futile attempt, imagining that when we returned two and a half months later, black tom would no longer be around.

We checked outgoing train schedules, airmailed Dr. Sellman when to expect the cats, took the nervously mewling crate down to Railway Express, and sent it out, with food and instructions, prepaid.

Thus was devised the system we followed for years. Dr. Sellman would hold them until we announced our arrival and send them along. We would ship them back and he would hold them until we could pick them up and take them to Piseco.

From time to time during that period, Dorothy and Johnny would try with a carefully plausible argument to talk me into taking them north in the car—a nest amid the luggage, mild tranquilizers, maybe collars and leashes for roadside relievings, smuggle them into motels. But I never fell into the trap of being obliged to come up with a logical refutation of each point. I merely expressed vast astonishment that two otherwise intelligent people could even pretend to propose such chaos.

I can imagine, for example, how they would react to leashes. Once we were able to give up the toilet-box-system on State Street and give them continuous access to the out of doors, we never saw them go, except very very rarely and then through the accident of taking a walk and coming across one of them in a remote place. It was a private and fastidious affair, one that they certainly would not undertake while at the end of a string.

. . . In the last couple of years the infirmities of age have at last led Roger to consider comfort more important than total privacy. Our screened terrace at Point Crisp is very large, with numerous planting areas full of peat moss and heavy growth. He began to use a far corner of it, behind a screen of dwarf banana. We have made it more suitable with a frequently replenished layer of kitty litter. Last Christmas Johnny and his wife, Anne, drove down from Michigan in a VW bus bringing their five cats with them—thus proving his nerves are better than mine have ever been—and they spent the holidays in our guesthouse. They had one adult cat, two almost adults, and two kittens. (The smallest female kitten was named Abishag after the biblical virgin taken into bed to keep the venerable king warm.)

Their cats were trained to kitty litter in big, shallow plastic pans. They put one in the guesthouse and one in the studio near the door to the terrace, which was propped ajar so Roger could get out there when the need arose. The weather was cold and uncomfortable for an ancient cat, and he was feeling unwell during the holidays. He took advantage of the convenience placed there for the new generation. As it had been almost eighteen years since he had used such a device, and because he is a very large cat, his first attempt was a total failure due to his getting only his front feet into the plastic bin. But from then on he was ept, and after the kids and their cat-colony had departed and the weather stayed cold, we continued the arrangement. When the weather warmed, Roger, by his own decision, reverted to his familiar area beyond the dwarf banana trees.

In addition, I knew exactly how the cats would react to a collar. When Geoff was small he was limply content to have our small boy dress him in improvised garments. Johnny also, without damage to his eventual unmistakable masculinity, owned a doll bed when we lived on State Street, and Geoff would sleep happily therein, head on the pillow, blankets tucked around him, a rather startling sight to come across in the living room when you were walking through with your mind on other matters.

As Geoff reached maturity, his attitude changed. He would endure having people put things on him, but it depressed and humiliated him. He would stand somewhat in the position of a steer with its rear end toward a blue norther, and look patiently, enduringly miserable. When he was disrobed or de-hatted, his relief was apparent.

Roger, on the other hand, has always been the clown cat. And has always relished attention. Having anything put on him was his signal to prance and race and show off.

That would have been our roadside tableau—Geoff standing utterly hangdog, and Roger deciding we wanted him to climb the leash hand over hand.

Regarding motels, I remembered too clearly a tale my sister told, of one night in a motel with Buckethead. The cat slept a couple of hours, awoke feeling all too spritely, having been shut up in the car all day. The room walls were of that kind of pressed composition board she could get her nails into. So she invented a game of running up the wall, springing backward into the air, turning, and landing in the middle of either Dorrie or Bill. In about twenty minutes of that, Buckethead had the whole show back out on the road, and Dorrie recalls that before they left Bill spent quite a while pressing the little triangular tear marks in the walls back to invisibility with his thumbnail.

I was obdurate. There were vast reaches of Georgia and the Carolinas sufficiently depressing without the tireless ululations of car-hating cats.

EIGHT

The cats had their first full summer at Piseco in 1950, and they were busy the entire time. In Florida they were more indolent. At Piseco there seemed to be a flavor of industrious self-importance about them. They would hurry in and eat and hurry out. They were working at the trade of being cats. Those summers, from 1950 through 1957, were the summers of their prime, when they were both at their heaviest, their pelts the glossiest, their agility and condition at peak. They ate hugely and with minimum selectivity and ran it all off. Always, at Piseco, their rich coats had an incomparable smell, a sweet, fresh, airy odor related in some way to washing which has been dried in the fragrance of a spring wind.

Their transient life kept their automatic control mechanism for the density of the coats in perpetual confusion. Before we left Florida, they would begin to shed winter coats, but the coolness at the lake would slow this process. Toward fall they would begin to grow a winter coat apparently planned for an Adirondack winter. They would come down then into the really suffocating heat and humidity of Florida in September, and, after a shocked pause, they would shed with such profusion our environment seemed adrift with cat hair which adhered to everything within range—furniture, clothing, and moist people.

We have one charming picture of the two of them that summer at the rented camp. Nephew John Gilbert Prentiss, Sam's younger, was about six years old, and, trolling along the lake shore with his father, he personally caught and boated a fine small-mouth bass a little over three pounds. I took his picture on the narrow front porch of the camp. John Prentiss wears a red shirt and a wide, proud grin. He holds up his big bass. One cat is on the railing beside him, looking at the bass with pleasurable anticipation, and the other winds around the boy's ankles, just the banner of the upright tail visible in the photograph.

Just before the school year started we drove on down to Clearwater Beach, to the house on Bruce, sent for the cats, and settled in. We fixed a window for them in a living-room corner which opened onto the carport. They made their thorough inspection of the area, inside and out, noting the food corner in the kitchen, selecting temporary sleeping places. Cats have the habit of sleeping in one place for a month or so, then changing to another place. When there are two of them, after a little while there are several cat-places where claims have been staked at one time or another.

This is as good a moment as any to describe one of the formal courtesies cats extend to each other. Reading about it in the cat book James and Pamela Mason wrote some years ago made us more aware of it. If a cat is on some comfortable elevation, such as a hassock, and the other cat wishes to join him, the other cat leaps up and asks permission by giving a lick at the face of the resting cat. Permission is expressed by a return of the lick, and the new arrival thereupon settles down. If the response is a sulky snarl or even a hiss, the visiting cat will leap down again and find some other place. This joint sharing of any restricted area was always more of a trial to Roger than to Geoff. Geoff pushed. He could push even when apparently asleep, exerting a continuous pressure. He filled up each inch he gained thereby, and kept right on pushing. He used this device on people as well as on brother cat. Many times we have seen Roger grant Geoff permission to join him only to find, twenty minutes later, that Geoff had worked him so near the edge his only choice was to jump down and walk indignantly away.

Cats have a habit of leaping up into the laps of those visitors least likely to enjoy providing comfort for a cat. Their nervous, habitual reaction is to stroke the cat. The cat interprets this as permission to settle down and does so immediately, then seems baffled to be set back down on the floor. If the cat is not touched he will quite often hesitate for a few moments and then jump back down of his own accord.

During the second or third evening of their residence at that house, both cats suddenly came catapulting back into the living room through their window from the night outside. Their tails were huge, spine hair ruffed up, and they ran in a half crouch. Never, before or since, have we ever seen them so frankly terrified. At Piseco they had sometimes come home in an unseemly haste after encountering some sort of goblin, but they seemed to make a pretense at indifference. This time they scuttled close to the people and whirled and stared back toward their window. The sound came out of the night, a great tomcat cry, savage, threatening, and of exceptional volume. Our cats flattened. The tom circled the house for some time, making chilling and explicit threats of murderous intent. We knew it was the big black one we had failed to trap.

Toms will kill male neuters who stray into their territory. They will also, on rare occasion, rape them. One night in Brookview, New York, Heathcliffe cat came home in hideous shape, dragging himself along. He had been mercilessly chawed and had so little use and control of his back legs, they thought he could have been clipped by a car and had his spine damaged. They took him to a vet who, after examination, said Heath had been raped by a

97

tom and had perhaps a fifty-fifty chance of recovery. He was a very sick and helpless cat for weeks and finally began to recover and eventually became entirely well.

We knew the black tom was a mortal danger to our two, so we closed their window, fixed a cat box for them, ignored their night pleas to be let out. We left the window open in the evenings while we were still up. They had responded so respectfully to the tom, we believed they would not wander far and would come racing back in at the first sign of danger. But we also suspected that if the house was dark and we were abed, the tom might very well come through their window to kill them in the house.

Two evenings later, just before Johnny's bedtime, the cats came dashing in through their window in panic, and the big black tom followed them right into the house, right into the living room where we all were. He was enormous and so intent on murder he did not even seem to notice us. I saw the chance to rid ourselves of the problem and circled quickly and slammed the cat window down. Only then did the tom realize he was trapped, and he ignored our cats completely. He raced swiftly around the room, a big, black, shadowy menace, looking for some way out. Our pair stood against the wall in awed silence, staring at the frightful intruder. Finding no way out, he raced down the long hallway which bisected the one-story house, and I saw him disappear into the darkness of our bedroom through the open door. I followed him, reached in and turned on the room lights, backed out, and closed the door. We were all awed, but Roger and Geoffrey most of all. They were both shaped like Halloween drawings, made not a sound, and moved very slowly, picking each foot up to an unaccustomed height and setting it down again with the care they might use if they were on a ledge a thousand feet in the air.

Dorothy, Johnny, and I had a conference, and we decided I had better kill it. It seemed the only practical solution, and I believe we arrived at it because I thought I had the means to do it with a minimum of fuss, mess, and difficulty. There was no legitimate firearm in the house. But I had a pellet gun, an air pistol with a built-in lever and plunger which, when pumped enough times, could build up a considerable force, enough to imbed the pellet into a board. Suspecting that it might stun him rather than kill him, I selected an additional weapon, a miniature baseball bat given Johnny by Frank O'Rourke, the writer, when we had lived on Acacia Street. If the pellet only stunned the cat, I would administer the *coup de grâce* with the bat.

Thus equipped for safari, with the other four members of the pride waiting anxiously in the hallway, I entered the bedroom and closed the door behind me. We had twin beds. I squatted and spotted the tom crouched under the further bed, staring toward me. I had loaded the pistol and pumped it up to its recommended maximum. It was quite accurate at short range. I knelt and aimed carefully under one bed and over to where the cat lay under the other. Its eyes glinted in the reflected lights of the bedroom. I felt slightly ridiculous, and had no relish for the job. The tom was an extraordinarily handsome animal, and quite the biggest cat of the house-cat breed I ever saw.

I aimed right between his eyes and about a half inch above them and fired. The cat gave a great twitch, a yowl of pain, rage, and warning, and with no slackening of agility moved further away. I reloaded, pumped, fired again with exactly the same result. I was merely torturing the poor, damned beast. I tried four or five more shots, getting as close as I could. I no longer felt ridiculous. I felt sick and helpless and disgusted with the idiocy of my brilliant idea. I decided I had better run him down with the bat. About ten seconds later he showed me how poor an idea that was. He came leaping from floor level, up through the narrow space between the twin beds, leaping right at my face, going for my eyes. I fell back and away and took a futile swipe at him, and he was back under a bed before the bat finished the swing. When he had hung for a moment in the brighter light in mid-air I had seen the old scars, the ragged edges of the ears, and a wet and matted place on his forehead above his eyes, a dark shine of blood in the black fur. Dorothy was calling questions to me through the closed door. I took out my frustration on her by roaring at her to leave me alone. She heard the squall of the cat at each impact and had heard me thudding around when he had jumped at me.

Once again I was back in the viaduct long ago. But that cat had been dying, and this one would not die. I tried two more shots and then suddenly saw after the leap and yowl that followed the second one that there was just one reflecting gleam of eye in the cat-blackness. My stomach turned over, and I went out into the hall closing the door behind me. "This goddam toy pistol," I said. "This lousy feeble stupid excuse for a . . ."

I must have looked just as miserable as I felt. Dorothy said, "If it isn't strong enough, maybe you'd better just open the screen in there and he'll go out."

I was tempted. I'd spent a long time in there. Maybe he'd heal, off in the brush. They wouldn't be honorable scars of combat. I'd been like some stupid bird, trying to peck him to death. And I was not going to tell her in front of my small son that Lieutenant Colonel MacDonald had managed to blind the cat in one eye, in a battle plan of remarkable stupidity. If he did recover, he'd be back. He had that look.

Then I admitted to myself how it had to be done, and I told her I'd hurt him too much to turn him loose, and I went back in. When I went in, he did a strange thing. He jumped into the air on the far side of the twin beds, not at me, but just up into the air, as high as my face and ten feet away from me, claws extended and white fangs showing, cursing me as he jumped.

It took me two shots to get the other eye. With that gone, he turned as utterly meek as the cat in the pond. In a low crouch he went to the wall and began a slow circuit of the room, staying close to the baseboard, making a thin keening sound of fright, searching some way out of this sudden total darkness. I moved to intercept him and swung the bat and struck him heavily on the broad tomcat skull. He dropped at once, quivered, and was still. His face was a terrible blankness of wet black fur. I went to the door, weak with reaction, opened it, and said, "Well, I guess I finally . . ."

Whereupon the tomcat made a horrid wailing sound and his long tail began to twitch. I ran back and hit him again.

He looked no smaller in death. Dorothy brought me a big, sturdy grocery bag. I grasped the end of his tail, using a paper towel to hold him with, and, holding the upright bag open with my left hand, I found I did not have an arm span long enough to raise him high enough to get him into the bag. Dorothy had to come and hold the bag open so I could lift him in. I did not weigh him. I was not interested in him as a trophy. He had to be over twenty pounds. I carried the bag out and put it in the trunk of the car and then came in to do something about the bedroom. The rug was almost wall to wall. The room had a strong pungency of tomcat, plus the other scents of death. His excrement had splattered the rug. Roger and Geoffrey tiptoed about in that room for all the world like spinster tourists inspecting a disaster area. Dorothy got Johnny to bed. We shooed the cats out, shifted furniture, rolled the rug up, and carried it out to the carport. Leaving Dorothy to the distasteful chore of scrubbing the area where he had died, I drove to the causeway which goes from the beach to the mainland, parked near the first bridge and walked out onto it with the heavy paper bag. It occurred to me that if any local law came cruising by they might think, from the shape and weight of my burden and from my furtive manner, that I was disposing of a human head.

After two cars went by, I dropped the bag into the bay, into the Gulf. I leaned on the railing for a little while. It was a hot night. It seemed strange to me that there should be such a residue of emotional exhaustion. It did not seem, to use the only expression I can think of, quite manly. Yet I had been through a war and had acquired a fairly precise knowledge of my strengths and limitations and had learned I could manage as well as the next man.

Yet, somehow, even today that grotesque slaying of the black tom is more vivid in my mind than much of the clattering, grunting, deadly inefficiency of men trying to slay each other. Perhaps war is such a profound implausibility, it provides its own insulation against reality. Those fearless eyes in black fur under the bed had been a reality which was perhaps in some telling resonance with the

101

drowning of the other cat so long ago. And perhaps a writer is curiously vulnerable to these subterranean relationships.

After the rug came back from the cleaners, apparently pristine, it was a long time before Roger and Geoffrey ceased tiptoeing in there to sniff at traces far too faint for the deadened senses of people.

This account makes Rog and Geoff sound far too girlish and timid. The three dog incidents while we lived in that house will bring them back into proper focus.

The first one made me laugh until I hurt. A chesty and self-important little dog lived directly across the street. I cannot recall him bothering Rog very much, but during our first few weeks there, whenever he spied Geoff out in the open, he would come barreling over at top speed, in full voice, and chase Geoff into the carport and up to his window ledge. Geoff would come in, all haired up, twice his normal size, his aplomb considerably shaken. He was not used to having dogs chase him, but somehow the one across the street had gotten the initial jump on him and kept pursuing the advantage with great enthusiasm.

Fortunately both Dorothy and I were in the living room the day Geoff decided how to handle it. Or, possibly, the decision was made because we had been there to witness his flight. At any rate we heard the frantic barking coming closer, and Geoff came in the window. He sat on the table inside the window and glowered out at the dog still barking in the carport. He stayed very swollen. Quite suddenly, and with the air of a man spitting on his hands before tackling a hard job, he went back out that window at full speed. For an astonished second the dog stared at the alarming apparition bearing down at him. He took one slashing slap across the chops, spun, and went kiyi-kiyi home, Geoff a step behind him. Geoff stopped at the edge of the street and sat and washed. From then on there was no nonsense from that dog. Sometimes, from a safe distance, he would bark, but he did not put much feeling or expression into it.

Later that season I heard some kind of commotion out

at the side of the house, and then a sustained wailing sound of heartbreak. Dorothy heard it too and we went out to investigate. There were young Australian pine trees there, planted in a row several feet apart. The grass had grown high under the trees, and the limbs sagged low. The trunks were about two inches thick. Roger sat washing about six feet from the tree, and Geoff was at about the same distance on the other side of the tree. Both of them looked entirely smug. The mournful complaints still came from the base of one tree. Peering under there, we saw a ruff of orange hair nestled down in between the grass and the tree trunk. Dorothy grabbed one cat and I grabbed the other and, to their displeasure, fed them in through their window and pulled it down from the outside so as to remove them from whatever the action was.

We went back to the tree, and I parted the grass and stared at what, from the color and the sound, I thought might be a Pekingese. The sad song stopped, and slowly and timorously, a full-grown collie unwound itself and stood up. It had been wrapped entirely around the tree trunk and had flattened itself into an incredibly small space. It was a young dog, though full-grown. It stared around, saw that the enemy was not in sight, then with tail tucked under, in total silence, it sped away through a neighbor yard and out of sight. We never saw it again. When we opened the window the cats came out and looked for it and seemed surly about the interference.

That same season, in the following spring, the cats put on a display of thoughtful co-operation which surprised and enchanted us. Though we saw much the same thing happen many times later on, this was the first time we had witnessed it. It was a hot day. Our neighbors had visitors. The visitors arrived with one of those little, unidentifiable dogs which have a shrill yapping bark and which bark constantly, apparently just for the joy of it.

It was a Sunday afternoon, and the constant shrill yapping got on our nerves before it finally began to bother the dozing cats. At last they went out together. There was a gap in the thick, high hedge dividing the property. Roger went strolling casually through the gap in the hedge, came to an abrupt and horrified stop, and arched his back as

103

though to say, My God, a Dog! Thereupon he whirled and ran for his life back through the gap and along the side of the house. The little dog chased him in furious glee. Roger led him past where Geoff was crouched in wait behind a bush. When Geoff sprang upon the small dog, Roger whirled and joined the fun. Between them they did not so much chase the dog back through the gap as bowl him along. The dog screamed. They sat on our side of the gap, washed for a little bit, and came back into the house and stretched out again. In the hot, lazy afternoon the little dog's whimpers died away, and there was a pleasant silence, a restful silence.

Before we went north for the summer in 1951, we decided to move further down the coast, down to the Sarasota area, where perhaps we could live on the water. Clearwater was beginning to show the commercial results of the enormous population pressure in the Tampa area, and waterfront was already at a premium which had taken it out of our reach. We knew by then Dick Glendinning, the writer, in Sarasota, and Sally. Dick helped us find a rental for the following season, on Casey Key opposite Nokomis. We rented a frame cottage on four hundred feet of gulf-to-bay land owned by Randy Hagerman, one of the owners of the Plaza Restaurant in Sarasota, stowed possessions there, and headed north.

NINE

—◆—

That was the first summer we spent in the new camp. It was a delight, for people and for cats. The south shore of the lake was more wild than the old shore where the camps were close together. We built on a rock ledge and had a cement deck overlooking the lake. Our road was over eight hundred feet long. It was and is a good place to live and work.

The cat window was in the front, opening out onto the cement ledge of the waist-high fireplace on the terrace.

Later, Roger was to discover that he could leap up under the shield and into the mouth of the flue. This was an idiot performance, and he would stay up in there, peering down, quite obviously very satisfied with himself. When it acquired a heavy coating of soot up in there he stopped. Cats do not voluntarily dirty themselves.

The flaw in the window arrangement was that they reached it from the inside by hopping up onto the glass-topped table in the dining end of the long kitchen, next to the wall of stone which was the back side of the living-room fireplace. Our cats were quite self-effacing about this exit system. Staying close to the wall they would hop to chair, to table, and glide out. By never giving an inch we had managed to train them never to hop up onto the table where the people were eating. They did beg scraps sometimes, but in a mild and mannerly fashion. Roger was the one who came closest to taking advantage. He would sit patiently on an empty chair and then, with the stealth of an awareness of guilt, he would put one paw on the edge of the table. His name said in a tone of accusation was usually sufficient to make him flatten his ears, gulp, and pull the paw back. When this did not work, you could commit the indecency of leaning forward and blowing into his face. He has always despised and resented this. He will stalk away, pausing to stare back two or three times. He manages to express incredulity and resentment. How can you possibly be so crude? Geoffrey never took such violent exception to it.

We did not mind the Piseco window arrangement. In fact, it was handy on those days so cold we did not want any window open. It could be readily reached to be opened for a cat and closed again.

But visiting cats and kittens made it a little less than ideal. I remember one time when Charlie, in momentary confusion, tried to leap from the floor to the window sill. Trouble was, there was a good solid hunk of plate glass in the way. He gave himself a thump that left a little knot on his head. For days he preferred to holler at the door to get in and out. And, summer before last, a visiting kitten, enormously busy, had the habit at mealtime of jumping up into a lap at the part of the table furthest from the window, scrambling onto the table, and charging through the groceries on his single-minded way out.

Roger has always had a precise awareness of his table rights. Circumspect about intrusion at any meal, he will nonetheless leap up onto the table without hesitation, when Dorothy is reading there or writing letters, and spread himself out amiably atop whatever she is trying to do.

Neither cat tried to steal anything from the table. With

one startling exception—the time Geoff got hooked on pills. But that comes later.

At Piseco I took wicked advantage of my increasing knowledge of cat psychology to cure Roger of a habit that was slowly driving Dorothy out of her mind. We had one of those sling chairs, or safari chairs as they are sometimes called, canvas with slots or pockets which fit over the four extremities of a frame made of bent and welded metal rod. The canvas was black. Roger thought it the finest invention of man, a perfect hammock to take the curled shape of a somnolent cat. And he left a thick deposit of gray hair against the black each time.

We had learned the curious uselessness of those chemical compounds designed to keep cats off things. One application was enough. They jumped up into the treated chairs, snuffed, moaned softly, jumped down, and threw up.

There seemed no way to keep Rog out of the sling chair. Then I had an idea. With fiendish Dagwood grin, I freed the two bottom pockets and placed them back *against* the metal rather than hooked over it, and fastened them there with Scotch tape. By then Roger was convinced it was his chair. The next time he leaped gracefully into it to settle down, it pulled loose and dumped him on the floor. He collected himself and strolled haughtily away. The next day he tried it again, with the same result, then never went near it again. A cat cannot abide being made to look ridiculous.

Though you could usually depend upon Roger and Geoffrey to respond in individual ways to the same stimulus, I recall one incident that first summer in the new camp when their reactions were identical. After what I shall call a jolly evening down in Utica with Eugene and Mary Hubbard, we drove back to Piseco, and I brought along Eugene's soprano saxophone, with a little book of elementary exercises thereon.

We were greeted warmly by the cats. I sat down and put my fingers on what I hoped were the right keys and tried a simple scale. There are few sounds less pleasing than those made by the novice saxophonist, and a soprano saxophone is the worst of all. After a few seconds of frozen horror, both cats began to howl like dogs, giving almost exactly those same ululations as when sad hounds bay the moon. When I stopped, they stopped. When I began again, they paced about in distress, howling, and then went out through their window into the night. I put the infernal machine away. I tried the next day and the next with the same result, and then I took it back to Eugene. I couldn't take that much criticism.

There was more wild life on the new side of the lake. There was a rock shelf eighty feet from shore not quite covered when the lake is at its highest and of considerable area when the lake is low. Ducks roost there. When we arrive there is always at least one merganser family, the ten or twelve ducklings riding on mother's back. We check on them throughout the summer, watching the dreadful attrition, seeing her at last with two or three who live to reach her size. Large migratory seagulls always rest there in the fall, loners who sit scruffily on the rocks, looking as if they were pondering whether such long trips are worth the effort. Wild Canada geese lay over in the shallow bay to the east of us, arriving and leaving with that incredible communal chortling which sounds like a D.A.R. convention after some scoundrel has spiked the punch.

The fine people who own the land to the east of us, the Leightons and the Zimmermans, have their place beyond the shallow bay and own the major share of the lake front between our camps. I own the rest. We are leaving it as is, and now it is the last place at our end of the lake where the wild things feel safe in coming down to the water.

Deer water there. We have not bothered them. If we happen to come too close, they trot a minimum distance and continue browsing on witch hopple. One year there was a doe with twin fawns, and their hoofmarks in the firm damp sand at the water's edge were dime-size, beautifully crisp, and perfect. There are red squirrels and chipmunks and white-foot mice, scarce one season, abundant the next. Some summers the bird book is used constantly; other years we have a few marsh sparrows, nothing more.

Porcupines have come onto the back porch at night to

gnaw the salty handles of the tools. There are fishers in the area, dark, long, heavy-bodied, catlike animals built close to the ground, and of such incredible speed and agility they can spot a red squirrel halfway up a tall tree and grab him before he can reach the branches too slender to bear their weight. Brown rabbits graze in the small open area behind the house.

I remember the day a few years ago when we got up at dawn to watch the television broadcast of the first time we put a fellow into the lower limits of space, in a sort of lob shot. We looked out the big window in the living room and saw a pair of otters down our shore line, playing some intricate game of amphibious tag. The one swam out to the rocks, dived, and caught a large chub, perhaps a pound and a half. He killed it and washed it and carried it ashore to the other one, and they shared it.

The next time I saw Sam Prentiss, I said, "There are some funny semantic values involved here, but somehow those otters seemed to me more *important* than heaving somebody in a piece of hardware a thousand miles across the ocean. In some nutty way having the otters show up seemed to make that space shot sort of sad and comical and artificial. And maybe pretentious."

Sam, with wry glance, said, "It's taking time, but you *are* learning."

We hear the shrill yap of the red fox. One of the standard amusements is to drive to the town dump at night, leave the headlights on, and watch the bears. They are the native black bear, up to six hundred pounds in weight. They have one magic I shall never understand. If you placed Roger cat on a loose 45-degree slope composed of cans, bottles, miscellaneous trash, he would make a rumpus akin to dropping bedsprings into greenhouses. But those big bears can drift across such a slope like a bulge of dark smoke, making not the slightest clink or rattle.

Homer Preston, the game protector for the area, is continuously apprehensive about tourists who go to see the bears, who get out of their cars and, conditioned by the myths of Disney and the bears' mild acceptance of being watched, might one day try to pet one. Homer knows that if this ever happens, the bear is going to pat right back

109

with an energy, speed, and force which could separate the tourists into two or three unattractive pieces.

Not long ago the New York State Conservation Department, in co-operation with Cornell University, conducted a three-year study of the large community of bears in the central Adirondack region. After sides of bacon and culvert traps had been used to catch them, they would then be knocked out by means of a hypo gun and, while unconscious, would be weighed, measured, tagged, and get one ear notched. In the case of the male bears, one testicle was removed and shipped in dry ice to the lab at Cornell. One can imagine that the male bears awoke in a state of some confusion. I believe about six hundred were trapped over the period of the study, and they discovered that the male bears are potent only on alternate years, one half their number being potent in any given year. During the off year their reproductive equipment is non-functional. Though the layman is not likely to get much conversational mileage from this discovery, I assume it must have stimulated the professionals vastly.

One summer not long ago, when the cats could not be with us, for reasons I must explain later, we fed a family of raccoons on the front terrace. For some time Dorothy had been feeding some unidentified creature, leaving a paper plate of scraps out behind the pump house at night. We had to go to New York City for a week, and when we returned the raccoons had become so anxious about the sudden cessation of the handouts, they came around to the front of the camp, a huge female who looked practically round, and her half-grown child. We would leave the outside floods on after they became bolder. We fed them puppy biscuits by hand, but this was hard on the nerves. Those front teeth are like chisels. They move very slowly toward the biscuit and then suddenly take it with an awesome snap.

(We had to stop feeding the red squirrels by hand when, one day, Dorothy walked out without peanuts and the irritable squirrel jumped from the cement deck up to her hand and sliced the pad of a finger open as if a razor had been used.)

One night when we were watching the two raccoons

110

through the window, a huge male raccoon came lumbering slowly up the three concrete steps at the end of the deck, and the female went waddling to meet him. We were certain we were going to see a vicious battle. Among most animals the females will drive the males away from their halfgrown young. She reached him just as he got to the top step, and they put on the most incredible greeting we have ever seen. They smooched shamelessly, nuzzling into each other's throats, rubbing heads, for at least a full thirty seconds, and then together came trundling to the food she had left. I have never seen this kind of display of affection between the male and female of any wild species. It was definitely not the practical business of checking each other's coats for scents, nor was it a shared washing or scratching, nor even a mating prelude. It was simply a very warm and happy hello.

(Sarasota County has been diligently eradicating the raccoons from the keys and the mainland for several years, on the basis of someone somewhere being bitten by a rabid one. Competent naturalists were quick to inform the county commission that rabies is endemic, relatively dormant, and in non-violent form in every sizable raccoon community in the world. They rarely infect other species, and it is one of the rarest of instances to have one of them go berserk. But minor agitation by the ignorant, the uninformed, the timorous, the nature haters who will not feel safe until the entire earth has been covered with asphalt, this minority gave the commissioners an excuse to set up a permanent patronage post of raccoon-killer, with an assistant to do the scut work, thus devising in perpetuity a nifty little way of rewarding the party hack who might foul up if given a more demanding position. Today a raccoon is a rare sight in the county, and the things the raccoons used to keep under control are beginning to create other problems, much to the bewilderment of everyone. I treasure the memory of the comment of one county commissioner who defended the eradication program by saying, "They are a very dirty animal.")

I tell of the wild life at Piseco to show what sort of natural community the cats had to adjust to in order to survive. There was violence out there in the woods. One night we heard some of it when we were awakened by loud sounds of vicious, snarling combat directly behind the camp, a prolonged thrashing, thumping, scrabbling, and then a sound of something going away through the woods swiftly, making heartbreaking cries of pain as it fled. When we investigated in the morning we found great wads of turf ripped up, small trees broken, but no print clear enough to tell us what it had been. Last summer, on the lake shore a few hundred feet from the terrace, we found a cat track which we photographed with a ruler beside it. It was an inch and a half wide and two inches long.

Had Roger maintained his dashing attitude, his willingness to stalk anything, this bravado combined with his general incompetence afield might have been a fatal combination. But somehow he acquired discretion in time. They became considerably less nocturnal on the wilder side of the lake. They would range further during the day, and stay much closer to the camp at nightfall. Roger violated this concept twice that first summer. Both times we had driven out after dark and came back home about midnight. It was the only time either of them showed any tendency to follow when we went out in the car. Both times we came back, and, way up at the head of the road, our lights picked up the gleam of Roger's eyes and he would come out of the brush. He hated riding in any car. But on both those occasions when we opened the car door, he came piling in, delighted to get out of the fearsome night and ride back down with us to the lights and safety of the camp.

Both of them acquired the same habit that first summer. It took us some time to check out what they were doing. If either cat, through carelessness, found himself an ominous distance from the camp when darkness fell, he would hole up rather than risk the trip home. They selected places in deep thickets of brush or down among the exposed root structure at the base of a tree. It happened less often to Geoff than to Roger. Apparently this sort of night would have such corrosive effect on feline morale, broad daylight would not give them sufficient heart to start back. By midmorning we would be tramping through the woods, calling the missing cat, each secretly convinced that this time

112

something had eaten him. The cat would come out of hiding, moving very cautiously, and then suddenly recover from the megrims and prance, dance, and game his way home to the greedy meal before the exhausted sleep. The other cat would always snuff at him carefully from head to tail, reading the clues of adventure.

While Sam and Evelyn, with kids and cats, were staying with us that summer, Geoff killed the weasel. It was mature, sizable, and had a very nasty expression. It was on the terrace, dead, when we got up. There was no mistaking who had killed it. Aside from the exploratory sniff, Geoff would permit no other cat liberties. And he seemed to realize that it is a rare and exceptional feat for a house cat to kill a weasel. They have a deadly swiftness. Whereas he would appear bored and indifferent about other species he lugged home, he was visibly impressed with this one. We gathered around to admire it and tell him what a beautiful cat he was. He kept bumping into our legs, purring, and going back time and again to the weasel to give it that little pat cats use to make the game wiggle one more time.

Later that day Sam skinned it, scraped the insides of the hide, rubbed salt into it and tacked it to a board to dry. In Clearwater we had become friendly with Alec Rackowe, the writer, and his wife, Gracie. Gracie's birthday was in the summer. Dorothy showed me a card she had bought for Gracie, one of those studio cards with a tag line that said, "What do you think? Mink?"

So we packaged the card with the weasel hide and mailed it to Gracie, reminding her that weasels in winter are known as ermine. It amused them. They had it on a hall table. The curing job which seemed adequate at Piseco was not up to the intense heat and humidity of Clearwater in midsummer. The first Alec knew of the problem was when a whole pack of dogs came to the front door and stood whining and grinning in at him through the screen, tails wagging. It was then he discovered he had a ripe weasel.

During the cool evenings that summer, the cats learned the special pleasure of a fireplace. At first the look of the flames fascinated them. Then they habitually cozied up to it. Geoff could endure more heat for a longer time than could Rog. When Geoff was finally forced to move back, his fur would feel almost too hot to touch.

When we began to pack to head south, we realized that the cats were becoming ever more aware of the significance of open suitcases and cardboard cartons. Though Geoff enjoyed settling down in any open container, both of them quite obviously related this particular activity to some pending unpleasantness. They would both become querulous, restless, irritable, spitting at each other, whining at the people. Geoff, usually so charmed to be toted about, would begin a mild, stubborn struggling when picked up, as though he detected a real possibility this might be the moment when he would be dumped into that damned shipping crate. And it became impractical to even try to pick Roger up. They were both fourteen-pound cats, and Roger could react like fourteen pounds of whirling fishhooks. They went back and forth through their window endlessly.

They expected the worst, and it happened, and we dropped them off at Dr. Sellman's with ear-weary relief.

TEN

———◆———

The last day of travel south was through torrential rains which were the aftermath of hurricane, rains which for the first time soaked through the tarp laced over our cargo trailer, and through the suitcases, washing the unnecessarily vivid colors out of the suitcase linings and onto the clothing therein.

We had written Randy when we would arrive, and it was raining hard that late afternoon when we got there, hardly in any mood to cope with the thousand irritating little problems involved in moving into a rented cottage. But Randy, bless him, had put a crew to work at the house. All the utilities were hooked up. The yard and house were spotless. Beds were made and turned down, opened packs of cigarettes on the end tables, Coke and beer in the refrigerator. Never have we been welcomed so imaginatively. A few days later when he came out to see how we were getting along, he brought a throw net, cast it over a fat mullet, split and cleaned the mullet on the dock, and showed Dorothy a fine method of broiling it.

The cats approved the setup at once. They liked the bay side. They would go over onto the beach when we did, but they did not care for it. The glare seemed to bother them. In all that open space they had no chance of catching a sandpiper, a sanderling, or a tern. They seemed to regard the surf as ominous indeed and would become agitated when we went out into it. They would pace back and forth and we could see their mouths make hollering motions.

We had seen a cat who had made an interesting adjustment to beach life. When we lived on Acacia Street, my sister and her husband had vacationed down at Madeira Beach. When we went down to see them there, Dorrie pointed out a cat at work. She had been watching him for days. A battered old timber groin extended out into the water. That cat would lie on the beach against the groin, in the actual wash of the surf. He looked like some wretched bit of flotsam, all soaked and caked, the waves washing over him. When finally some unwary water bird came near enough that sodden cat would spring and bring it down, kill it immediately, and carry it off the beach up into the sea oats to eat it. I have never heard of another cat who used this hunting scheme so contrary to cat habit and instinct.

At Casey Key that season we witnessed a triumph of cat co-operation which Roger and Geoffrey never again topped, at least not for an audience.

There were raccoons in the mangrove and water-oak thickets on the bay side. Our bay shore had been cleared. The thickets began at either side. A narrow dock extended straight out into the water. Dorothy had wanted to feed the raccoons some chicken skin, so she threw it out into the shallow water.

She called me to the kitchen that afternoon to see the raccoon. He was a dozen feet from the bay shore and in about six inches of water. It was low tide. His soaked legs gave him a skinny look. He was fumbling around on the bottom with his clever brown hands, finding the bits of skin, putting them in his mouth. When he searched by sense of touch alone, he would survey the bay shore, turning his head back and forth, evidently aware of resident cats.

Suddenly we saw Roger skulking quite carefully down through the tall grass which grew around the uprights to a short wooden water tower on the left. He settled down into the grass, out of our sight and apparently out of sight of the raccoon.

Then Geoffrey appeared from the left. He came ambling across the open yard behind the house. The raccoon froze, staring at him. We could not believe that Geoff was unaware of the raccoon not forty feet from him. Geoff acted goofy. He pounced at some small grasshoppers. He went up onto his hind legs like a kitten to bat at a yellow butterfly. We decided that the mighty hunter was putting on a pretty sorry performance. There was an upended boat at the right side of the yard. When Geoff, taking his idle time, disappeared from the raccoon's view behind the boat, the raccoon started eating again. And Geoffrey, suddenly swift, tense, and utterly businesslike, flattened out and crawled along the yard, staying close to the boat, keeping the boat between him and the raccoon. He stopped when he reached the end of the boat and stayed there, the end of his tail flicking.

Suddenly Roger came galloping out of cover, right down toward the shore. The startled raccoon took off, angling in toward the shore, herded in that direction by Roger. At just the right moment, Geoff dashed out to intercept him. Roger was gaining. The raccoon slowed for just an instant, just long enough for Roger to wind up and give him such a mighty thump on the back flank with his right paw, we heard the impact in the house. Raccoon sped for the mangroves. I think Geoff got one whack at him, too, but I cannot be certain. They made no attempt to follow him into the thicket. They stopped, sat in neighborly fashion, and began to wash.

In retrospect the utterly astounding thing was the absolutely calculated act Geoffrey had put on. See the happy cat? The cat is harmless. The cat is playing with bugs, see? The happy, stupid cat does not even know you are there. Roger had performed well too. Somehow he'd found the sense to wait until Geoff was in position before making his move.

It was at Casey Key that both cats adopted the practice of following me over to the beach when I carried a fish rod and tackle box. If I went over empty-handed, I went alone. On the beach side they would drowse in the shade of the sea grapes beyond the sand and watch me. As soon as I got a fish on, they would come strolling down to see what it might be. I caught a lot of little trash fish off that beach. They would sit and watch me bring it in. If it was a trash fish, a little jack, or a blue runner, I would filet it immediately, rinse the two halves in the Gulf, and give them each a half. After one attempt they had learned the futility of trying to eat raw fish in the dry sand. Tails bannered high, they would walk back up off the beach and settle down in the grass, eat the fish, tidy up, and wait for the next strike. They seemed to understand about people fish. When I caught something we were going to eat, put it on the stringer to clean later, and made the next cast, they would go back to the shade. It always seemed to distress them when I took the rod and tackle box and went the wrong way, got into the boat, and went off into the bay. As long as I could see the dock, I could see them sitting there. When I came back in, when I was still a good distance from the dock, I would see them trudging down from the house.

At that Christmas time in 1951, we were made forcibly aware of the presence of ex-house cats in the brush. They found they could come in the cat window and find food in the kitchen corner. The wrapped presents were under the tree. We went out one night and came back to find the living room filled with the unmistakable tang of tomcat. We tracked it down and found that the tom or toms had staked out our Christmas presents. We opened them that year at arm's length. A few nights later I heard a noise in the house and got up and turned on the light and watched three strange cats shoot past me and speed out the cat window.

We tried shutting the cat window at night. At intervals during the night our cats would take turns demanding service, and somebody would have to stagger out and let one or the other of them in or out. The twin beds were Hollywood beds without headboards, and the heads of the beds were even with the bedroom window sills. One night I merely unhooked the bottom of the screen and pushed it out, pushed the demanding cat out through the gap, and let the screen swing back. Dorothy suggested, and I agreed, that it was a pretty stupid compromise. We'd have cats walking on us all night long. Roger was the sort of cat you don't want in bed with you. Geoff would settle down. But Roger was and is a yaffler. I believe James and Pamela Mason invented the word. It applies to a cat which gets on your bed and begins such a noisy, spirited job of washing itself it shakes the bed and makes a pronounced yaffling sound. (Rhymes with waffling.)

But in an extraordinarily short time I could let cats in and out all night long without ever waking up. When they tramped across me, I'd push at the screen, and when they hollered outside, I'd hold the screen out and they'd leap to the sill. It seemed damned undignified to be the abject doorman for a pair of cats, but the arrangement worked the rest of the time we were there. They used their window during the days. Whenever we tried leaving it open at night, we had strangers in for a snack and for loud, emotional serenades.

It was there that some cat put a ragged edge on one of Roger's ears. He was always covered with scars and scabs under the chin from being mercilessly bitten by small rodents. But this was a visible memo of combat, worn jauntily, rather like a dueling scar acquired at Heidelberg.

It did not give him greater dignity. At seven years, by the standard cat-human ratio, he was nearing fifty. But if you were walking with him, he would suddenly break into a run, go fifteen feet up a palm bole at top speed, then hang there and peer down at you with a maddened gleam in his eye.

It was at the Casey Key house that I stepped on him. I was opening a door and he was underfoot and I stepped back, stumbled upon him, came down with my hard heel on his right front paw in such a way I could not, for a moment, get my weight off him. He screamed bloody murder. I broke no bones, but I did split the pad in one place. The foot became badly swollen, and then it became infected. It turned into such a bad infection that the veterinary had to open it up and put a drain through it from top to bottom. He suffered visibly. He limped pitifully. And it would irritate me beyond measure to have him walk toward me, pause, give me a baleful glance, then make a wide half circle around where I was standing. He held a grudge.

In a matter of weeks he was completely healed. The last sign of any favoring of that front foot disappeared. He was as speedy as ever and, to all appearances, had forgiven me.

But for a full year, and this I swear is true, if I offended that cat by, for example, scooping him off some place where I wanted to sit and setting him down on the floor, that con artist would look at me with unmistakable scorn, and then slowly and sadly he would *limp* away.

There was one foolish trick I started doing with him that year. He hated it and yet it intrigued him. When he was stretched out on some slippery surface, like the waxed floor of the kitchen, I would bend over him and put one hand on one side of him and one on the other and spin him like a propeller and, with one finger on the nape of his neck, keep him going for a few moments. It gave him vertigo. He would get up and wobble around and look as if he was trying to gag. He would leave the room and, moments later, come right back and flop down on the floor in front of me and look up expectantly.

You could not do that sort of thing to Geoffrey. He would have endured it in good spirit as he endured everything the people did, but he would not have understood.

That spring I did well enough professionally so we began to think of having a Florida house. A few years of rentals can make you feel you are being nibbled to death. I told Dorothy to go house hunting for something we could hang onto for a few seasons, furnish cheaply, and then unload. She looked for days and found a new house on Siesta Key, the last house on a small peninsula called Point Crisp, which sticks out into little Sarasota Bay.

We bought it before we went north. We've been there ever since, adding first a guesthouse, then an extension to the main house. For those six years—1952 through

1957—the cats shared our follow-the-sun life, and the cat things which happened seem to belong to one familiar place or the other, rather than to a specific year. Both places were familiar to the cats, the windows and the kitchen corners and favorite places remembered in the first minutes of arrival.

ELEVEN

There was the memorable instance of the big wave. When weather and tides were opportune, I used to knock off work in the late afternoon, take some frozen fishing shrimp out of the deepfreeze and with rod and gear take the narrow path through the three hundred feet of mangrove out to the sand bar at the end of Point Crisp and fish the dredged channel near the Inland Waterway marker.

On one strange afternoon I caught sixteen fish, each of an entirely different species. The cats would invariably accompany me, walking along with me, tails pleasurably high. They liked it much better than the beach. They would sit behind me like a pair of dogs, and when the line tightened and the reel hummed they would stand up and move closer, as eager to see what would come out of the water as I. The people in small boats thoroughly enjoyed it. A lot of them snapped our picture. I wonder how many of those pictures are tucked away in drawers and albums in the north, showing "that fellow fishing with those two big gray cats."

One afternoon the fishing was slow, and both cats lay on the shells a dozen feet behind me. I always wore old sneakers and pants so I could wade around on the submerged part of the bar. A cabin cruiser came up the channel from the south. It did not seem notably large or notably fast, but as it went by I noticed it was dragging a wake behind it worthy of a Great Lakes ore boat. It slapped me at about mid-thigh, and I turned, too late to scramble for my tackle box. Roger, for once, was more alert. He went scampering to high ground with the wave in close pursuit. Just as Geoff sprang up, the wave hit him and knocked him down and rolled him over. He came up sputtering, and as the wave drained off the shells, he headed miserably for home. He gave a tired whine of complaint about every twenty feet until I could no longer hear him.

Thereafter he did all his waiting up on the high ground. Roger braved the shell beach as before. When a fish was being caught, Geoff would come down to the edge of the water as before, but if while awaiting his share he happened to see a boat coming from any direction, even a skiff with a five-horse outboard, he would whirl and run to high ground, returning well after it had passed.

Actually, Geoffrey was bolder about the water than Roger. One year we began to find the tails and the bills of small needlefish by the cat dishes. It puzzled us. There were small needlefish, sometimes called ballyhoo, in the shallow bay waters on either side of the house. It was some time before we actually saw Geoff in the act of catching them. The shallows behind the house were flat calm. These small fish swim right on the surface. Geoff had waded out to his armpits and belly hair, and he stood absolutely motionless, ears cocked forward. As we watched him he gave a sudden snap at the water, and came out with a four- or five-inch needlefish in his jaws. He walked around the side of the house, came in his window with it, went directly to his dish, dropped it, put his foot on it when it flapped, and then neatly ate all of it but the bill and tail, and went back out and waded slowly into the bay.

Also, at Piseco, Geoff was the one who owned a frog. Every so often, all one summer, Geoff would go down to the lake shore and hop from rock to rock along the shore, pausing on each one to reach down into the water with one foot and feel all around the underside of the rock. Sooner or later he would find it, scoop it out, take it in his jaws and bring it up onto the terrace and put it down, and then purely hop the bejaysus out of it. We knew it was always the same frog, not only because of the markings but because, as the summer progressed, it became increasingly defeated and shopworn. He would give it gentle little taps on its rear end with one urging paw and admire the jumps until at last, when the frog was too dusty and dispirited to provide further entertainment, Geoffrey would walk away and one of us would take the frog down to the lake shore and drop it back into the water. If I remember correctly it was still in residence when we left, but one can imagine that it was terribly tired of cats. The next year Geoff spent quite a lot of time feeling around for it under the rocks before he gave up the search.

Once, at Point Crisp, Roger got very incensed at a large and scruffy-looking osprey. It was acting so strangely, I do not think it was well. Ospreys are of the hawk family, with a very cold eye, a big, wicked, tin-snip beak, and powerful, oversized talons designed to grab fish on the surface and fly off with them. The osprey landed on top of the telephone pole near our garage, and Roger spotted it. He yammered at it to come down and face the fierce cat, and when it ignored him, he managed to climb up onto the roof of the attached garage. This put him so close the bird got tired of listening to him and flew down to our back beach, Roger after him. By the time we got out there they were twenty feet apart. Roger was giving him that cat ballad generally reserved for night-calling cats, but he had no intention of getting any closer. The bird looked as if it wished he would get closer, just close enough. Thinking it might be ill, we immured Rog in the house, and I went to inspect the bird. I got to within ten feet and decided that was as near as I cared to get. It flapped off, flying not very well, but well enough to disappear over the key to the south.

During the evenings each spring, Roger and Geoffrey would go over to the house of Al and Connie Sheen, our nearest neighbors, to serenade Caffeine, their orange and white girl cat. It was ritual. They were both male neuters, and Caffeine was a spayed female, but cats seem to respond to some spring rhythm more persuasive than any specifics of ability. Caffeine, inside her screened cage, would respond with her own song. Geoff was the more loyal suitor. When, each year, their attentions ended, we would often see Caffeine by day, coming across the lot between our houses, apparently feeling that spring had not lasted long enough.

One summer at Piseco Dorothy heard some inexplicable thumping and thudding in the middle of the night and, realizing it had been going on off and on for some time, went to investigate. She found that the cats had gotten into a nest of baby rabbits, had brought them in, and, unaccountably, had been eating them in the shower stall. The mother rabbit is the only wild mammal in this country which will make absolutely no attempt to either defend her young or mislead predators. Realizing that bits of baby rabbit would be a horrid thing for children to come across in the morning, she cleaned the mess up then and there. The following morning when she was in the bathroom she looked into the shower stall and there, on the floor, saw one lone rabbit eye staring eerily back at her. At such moments it is very difficult to be fond of your house cats.

At Point Crisp we found we had some very unpleasant-looking rats living in the tops of the cabbage palms. Geoff grabbed one and brought it in and let it go in the hall, and it ran into Johnny's room and up the draperies and sat on the top of the drapery fixture, squeaking. Geoff looked at it for a moment, then went out to see what might be in his dish. He seemed to be saying, "There's a rat for you. Have fun."

We grabbed him and shoved him into Johnny's room and closed the door. He began an immediate complaint to be let out. He had no further interest in the rat. Nor could we interest Roger in it.

Johnny and I armed ourselves with a broom and the dubious pellet gun and went into the bedroom. We looked and looked and we could not find the rat. Yet there was no way it could have escaped. So we began a rat hunt. When you hunt a rat you do not stick your hand behind books and feel around for him. Finally we had looked everywhere except the bed, and when we began to take that apart, a rat-sized hump began to move back and forth erratically under the blanket. I raised the broom to give it a mighty swat, but Johnny yelled no and asked me what I thought his bed would be like if I hit it. So we prodded it out, and it ran over to a chair beside the white plaster wall. It paused for a moment near a chair leg, and I shot it, expecting no result at all. The pellet hit it in the throat. It sprayed an astonishing amount of blood halfway up the wall, ran in circles spraying at random, then collapsed and died in a little red puddle.

Geoff released another one in the kitchen another year, a young one. It hid in the back of the underside of the deepfreeze behind the coils and compressor. With a flashlight I could see it back there, but I couldn't get it out. When we thought it had left, we found it had moved into comfortable quarters under the dishwasher. There was a hole in the base of the dishwasher some three inches square. The cat-food corner was handy. So was the counter top. The rat would come out at night and haul astonishing quantities of food away, back into his nest. When I finally trapped him, using a huge rattrap with raw bacon lashed to the trigger, he had grown so huge the trap was just a damned inconvenience that sent him clattering around the kitchen in the middle of the night, unable to fit himself back through his hole. I got up and killed him with a fireplace poker, Geoff purring approval.

One day on Point Crisp a big, elderly fox squirrel fell off a telephone pole. Our neighbors, Dot Rhoades and her daughter, Judy Currier, asked our help. Johnny brought him home in a box. The squirrel seemed very feeble, and his muzzle was so white it looked to me as if he was expiring of age rather than illness. For a time it looked as though he might recover, and then he died, and before burying him I snipped off his magnificent tail and put it on a high place to dry. When it was ready, Roger was absolutely mad about it. By that time, Geoff, aside from the occasional solitary game, usually of his own devising, was not very impressed with playthings. He would play for a short, busy time with anything stuffed with catnip, and then, with the precision he had learned on Adirondack mice, he would open it up and eat the contents.

But the squirrel tail fanned old memories in Roger. Long ago he had been given one by Johnny. Dorothy had discovered that if cat toys were taken away from them and put away, the enthusiasm was renewed when they were produced again.

She is a light sleeper. She woke up in the middle of the night in Clearwater to the sound of a drawer being opened stealthily. And then another. With remarkably poor judgment, she did not awaken me, but instead sprang out of bed, went quietly to the doorway of the nearby living room, and snapped the lights on. Roger, blinking in the sudden light, sat on top of a breakfront desk. Several of the small drawers were open. The drawer pulls were of that type formed of a length of wood with a groove on the underside. As she watched him, Roger turned his paw over, hooked the underside of the drawer and pulled it open. He dipped his head in, picked up the squirrel tail, and jumped down off the desk. He had smelled it in there, but it had taken him a little time to find the right drawer.

At Point Crisp he was delighted to be presented with a new one. He savaged it for hours.

There was a year Geoff nearly died, the year we thought he had. Quite suddenly he began to act peculiarly. We took him to a very good veterinary, Dr. Ezekiel Thomas, located a few minutes away on the South Tamiami Trail. Dr. Thomas told us he was one very sick cat, running a high fever. He gave him a shot, decided he would be better off at home, and gave us pills to give him.

We should have closed the cat window. He went out and he didn't come back. Johnny was away at school. Dorothy was just out of the hospital. We hunted for him into the night, calling him, then slept poorly and began the hunt the next morning.

In the afternoon I spotted him under our guesthouse. It is of post-and-beam construction, elevated on four-foot piers. He was under there in the shade, panting. I called him, and there was no response. I should have gone under there immediately, but instead I went part way back to the main house, calling to Dorothy that I had found him. When I turned back it was just in time to see him moving slowly into the heavy brush beyond the guesthouse. I ran after him, but he had disappeared completely. A heavy mangrove jungle three hundred feet long and a hundred and fifty feet wide is an impossible locale for any detailed search. We did the best we could. After three more nights and days, after the grisly watch for buzzards over the mangroves, we were very depressed people, wondering how in the world we would write Johnny to tell him Geoff was gone for good.

During the evening, on the fourth night, we heard a faint, frail mew. Geoff came slowly through the cat window. I cannot guess how he managed to leap to the outside shelves because he was so weak that he had difficulty walking. He was down to six skeletal pounds. He drank a little warm milk, ate a very small morsel of warm hamburg, and went exhaustedly to sleep in a comforting carton beside Dorothy's bed. When Dr. Thomas examined him again he said that the cat had somehow gotten over the worst of it and would most certainly recover.

We should have guessed that he would go off by himself when mortally ill. In that sense he was a more primitive animal than Roger. Roger, even when slightly ill, makes outrageous demands for attention, suffers visibly with thespian art, and wants to stay as close to people as he can get.

The one thing that made us so happy he came back was that cat's special capacity for love. No one ever got up in the night to go to the bathroom in our house without having Geoff stir himself and come lumping in to sit in the darkness and lean against a leg, a small, warm furnace of purrs. He was not demanding food or amusement or a chance to move to the people-bed. He would merely come in and say hello, and then stump on back to wherever he was sleeping at the time.

After his illness he slept a great deal and ate hugely. His strength and energy came back quickly. Dorothy took advantage of a curious craving that cat had. There had been a previous time when Johnny, recovering from an illness, was supposed to take brewer's-yeast tablets, eight of them with each meal. When Dorothy set the table, she would put the eight tablets by his plate. Certain confusions began to arise. He would say she hadn't put them there. She would swear she had and accuse him of taking them and forgetting he had. One day Geoff was caught in the act of reaching a stealthy paw onto the table and hooking the tablets off and gobbling them. We ran a test. He adored them. We would put a dozen on the kitchen floor, and Geoff would vacuum them up, chomping each one before swallowing it. Roger, interested in what Geoff was eating so greedily, snuffed at a tablet and then backed off and tilted his head and looked at the brother cat as if he suspected Geoff of some kind of insanity.

During his recuperation, I think Dorothy gave that cat enough brewer's yeast to keep Gussie Busch going for months.

After he had learned the delights of the stolen tablets and had been given some of his own, you had to be careful not to shake any kind of pill bottle or candy jar or Geoff would spring up from sleep and trot to the kitchen, looking pleased and expectant.

Also, he was the only cat I have ever seen who liked apricot juice.

TWELVE

To dwell only upon incidents is, in a sense, misleading, because these incidents do not show how these house guests, even after maturity, continued to change in interesting ways.

For years Dorothy and Roger carried on a most curious and stubborn conflict. Things have to be done to cats. Drops for itching ears. Powder for flea time. Nails on many-toed feet tend to sometimes grow back upon themselves and start digging into the pad. Matted hair must be brushed. When cats have colds, their eyes need wiping.

Geoffrey was a stoic about these attentions. He endured them, and they were over quickly, and he bore no ill will. Roger was determined that no one was going to touch him without getting clawed ragged, and Dorothy was just as determined that he would learn to accept these necessary attentions. He would lie on his back and snarl and yowl at her, digging and biting every chance he got. I kept telling her that the cat might really hurt her some time. She was always dabbing medicine on the little nicks and gashes he gave her. For years it was stalemate. She wouldn't quit trying, and he wouldn't quit trying to make the whole thing impossible.

Then, over quite a comparatively short period, he mellowed. He became tractable. He became, in fact, so ingratiatingly gooey and sloppy that he began to be known as Gladys. Though still showing the wistful urge to let someone have it, he endured unwelcome and sometimes quite unpleasant attentions. It became standard practice, when they were ended, for him to go right to his dish and wait for something special, a reward for exemplary behavior. I can account for the change which occurred only by attributing it to the eventual, reluctant exercise of reason. No matter how venomous the objection, the unpleasantness, such as the removal of a tick, would be accomplished. He did not become "tamed" in the sense of being broken to obedience. He made the rational decision to accept, and this carried over to the ministrations of veterinaries also.

At Point Crisp he showed at one point an unmistakable capacity for logical thought. When we made the addition to the main house, we removed the garage, put in a double carport, and put my work area on top of the carport as the only second-story portion of the house. The sliding glass windows above my desk area open onto a shallow screened porch. From the farthest corner of this screened porch, one can look down at an acute angle directly into the window over the kitchen sink.

It was and still is Roger's habit to come up the stairs and pay me a visit on the average of about once every two or three days. Though he has never had Geoff's affinity for boxes, he has had an exploratory interest in cupboards. I have dozens of them in my work area, at floor level. He comes up and picks a cupboard, tugs tentatively at it with his claws, turns, and makes a small yow of polite request. Sometimes there is no vocalization at all, just the movement of the mouth. I get up and open it a few inches. He likes to pull them open the rest of the way. He goes in and explores. He isn't after game. He just wants to check and see what it's like in there. He doesn't settle down. He prowls around and leaves.

One day he wanted to go out on the screened porch. He had been out there before. On the day in question I let him out. As it was a warm day Dorothy had the kitchen window open, and she happened to be at the sink. When movement caught her eye, she called up to him. I watched him. He stopped and stared down at her, six feet away. He tilted his head and stared at her. She continued to talk to him.

Abruptly and purposefully he turned around and came back into my office, walked diagonally across to the stairs, went down the stairs to Dorothy's studio, walked back through the service area to the kitchen door and stood there and stared at her.

Nothing unusual here. However, that cat with the two of us observing him, repeated that trek *seven* times, without side trips, interruptions, or any lagging of attention and curiosity. Obviously the spatial relationships baffled him. Down there was the familiar food corner, the accustomed voice and greeting. There could not be a duplication. Yet how could he come so far yet remain so close? Seven times he stood on the porch and stared down at her. Seven times he went to the kitchen doorway and checked. It was not a game of hide and seek. He was doing no prancing. He was involved in solemn thought. At last he seemed satisfied, and when I next spotted him about fifteen minutes later he was sitting out in the sun in the driveway, either by accident or intent, in the precise place where he could most readily see both the upstairs porch corner and the downstairs kitchen window.

There was one interesting change of habit and attitude which seemed to be a result of the mellowing of old Turtlehead. When he decided once and for all that no harm was intended him, he went overboard in expanding the number of people he would trust. It was as though, discovering his own capacity for good will, he could now assume everyone felt the same.

Previously they had both been prone at times to pay visits. When we had people in the guesthouse, they would

133

spend as much time there as at the main house. They both quite obviously enjoyed the excitements and confusions of parties we gave. Geoff in particular was the party cat, showing off shamelessly, and very deft at singling out those guests who would most willing share the hors d'oeuvres. In his younger years I would do a party trick with him to demonstrate his trust and his amiability. I would take his hind legs in one hand, adjusting the grip carefully so as to avoid hurting his legs. Then I would lift him by the back legs and hold him at arm's length. He would hang there, apparently quite content, front legs extended, even purring at times. Trying the same thing with Roger would have been like trying to juggle a few nests of hornets.

Incidentally, one of Geoff's homely pleasures was to lie on his back in the shell driveway, wriggling, feet in the air and have somebody grasp his feet, front paws in one hand, rear ones in the other, and rub him back and forth on the shells, like a furry iron on a gritty ironing board. Roger's response to this was to try to get his teeth into the nearest wrist, not in anger but in too vigorous a response to what he thought an invitation to roughhouse.

Also, both of them seemed to feel that we employed people for the express purpose of amusing the cats. For several years we had a yard man they were especially fond of. Mac was a Negro with a miraculously green thumb and an extraordinary sense of design and proportion. He had such an affinity for growing things, that when he worked around the place he actually talked to the plants. And when he was at our house, the cats were in the middle of everything he did. Later it turned out that his habit of keeping his cigarettes in his hip pocket was a fatal one. During an argument he was shot through the heart when he reached for them.

He was replaced by Arnett Baker, the husband of Rianner Baker, who has been our part-time cleaning woman from the first year we lived there. The cats knew that dusters, dustcloths, and dry mops were game things. It took Rianner some time to get used to one of Roger's habits. He still does it, though rarely. He is stretched out on the floor in apparent indifference. If you walk within range, he reaches out and hooks you by one leg. If you are wearing pants, he uses the claws. Bare legs get a quick little tug when he hooks his arm around the ankle.

This would startle Rianner almost as much as the unexpected bite. Housework was punctuated by little gasps and yelps. Until she got used to him, I think he managed to upset her considerably. She was immediately fond of Geoffrey cat and intrigued and impressed by his responsiveness, which seemed like courtesy. Geoff was never too busy to say hello. If you walked by him twenty times in an hour, you would invariably get a greeting, a little noise which I can spell out as Yop. And whenever you opened a door for him to let him in, as he walked by you he would say his version of thank you, a strange little mumbled sound he uttered on no other occasions. A little Mermph, spoken with rising inflection.

I might interject here, about this business of opening doors, as the cats grew more elderly they would use their window when the people were unavailable. But it was an extra effort, and when there was the opportunity of doorman service, they used it.

Rianner, in time, became very amused by Roger and eventually fond of him. But he still complicates her chores. He is especially intrigued by mop water. He likes to trot behind in it while the floor is being mopped. He enjoys lying down on a damp, freshly mopped floor or, even better, a floor freshly waxed. He gets very excited over the odor of Clorox. Geoff was indifferent to it. But to Roger that odor seems to have some kind of sexy import. Perhaps it does bear some faint chemical relationship to the odor of tomcat. But he makes a ridiculous spectacle of himself weaving around and around a bucket of Clorox water, smirking and bumping his head against it.

Having mellowed, Roger became an inveterate caller. Alone, he would visit every house on the small peninsula, thumping the screen doors, walking happily in and making a short tour of inspection, tail high. If food was offered he would accept a little graciously, but that was apparently not his objective. There are just six houses. His last stop would be the house of Bruff and Beth Olin, the house on the point nearest the mainland part of the key. There, in addition to the house, he would go out onto the dock and hop aboard their cabin cruiser and check that over. Tour finished, he would come back down the road.

One year, right after the house next to Olins' had been rented, the woman there saw Beth in her yard and came over to tell her what had happened the previous afternoon, late. She said that a poor mother cat, obviously expecting kittens any moment, had come to the back door and asked to be let in. Once in, the cat had searched all over the house, obviously looking for a place to have the kittens. The woman had called the vet and had been told to fix a box for the cat. The woman had torn up one of her dresses to make a soft nest. The mother cat seemed to appreciate the box, purring and all, but then she began to ask to get out of the house. They had kept taking her back and putting her in the box, but finally she grew so insistent, they let her out and she hadn't been seen since, and the woman was very worried about her.

Beth, suddenly suspecting what had happened, asked the woman to describe the cat, and when she came to the part about something being wrong with its left eye, Beth said, "Oh, for heaven's sake, that was Roger MacDonald!"

As male neuters grow old they develop a loose and heavy fold of flesh under the abdomen. To the uninitiated, it could look somewhat like pregnancy. We are glad she did not rush poor old mother cat down to the animal shelter.

It must have been one of Roger's more confusing social experiences.

During those years we noticed that Roger's left eye began to reflect light in a different way than the right one did. It grew increasingly milky and opaque. One night, when a young eye surgeon was at a party at the house, he took a look at it and diagnosed it as a traumatic cataract, probably the result of a little nick or scratch received when the cats were engaged in fierce mock battle. He said that because of the cause, it was not likely to spread to the other eye. We could detect only one way in which it seemed to bother him. When he wanted to go out into the night, he was more cautious about going out through the opened door. It took him a little longer to decide that there was nothing out there which intended to eat him.

During the day his benignity and lack of suspicion made him a little foolhardy. He would climb aboard every service truck which parked there, from the phone-company truck to the plumber's truck, and we were afraid that while he was delving around among the tool boxes he might be driven away.

I suspect that there is no occupation in our civilization which entitles a man to more irritability than being a mail carrier at Christmastime. Yet one year, three times during Christmas week, Dorothy saw our mail carrier hop out of his truck, scoop the fool cat out of the drive, and carry him over and set him down in the shade of the pine hedge so he could turn his truck around without running over him.

The times were changing. The cats and the people were changing. Johnny went away to school at fifteen, to Oakwood School up in Poughkeepsie. When he came home for vacation and went away again, Geoffrey would search the house for him, making the calling sound, as in cat to cat, and pick Johnny's bed as his sleeping place for a time.

With Johnny gone, Dorothy began again to paint more frequently, with Roger as content to hop up and sample paint water as he was to follow the watering pail and drink from the terrace flower pots.

Intensive writing over a long period of time is exhausting in ways I find difficult to describe without sounding somewhat precious about it. You feel disenfranchised by reality, a half step behind and off to one side of your own skin, your view oblique, with most possibilities of genuine reaction cooled by being filtered through the habitual appraisal mechanics of your trade. You find an off-hours world crammed with the enticing stimulations of good books, good art, good conversation, but that creative effort necessary to these appreciations is too much akin to the process that uses you up in your work, and so, too often, aware of sloth and guilt, you surrender to the undemanding unvarying flatulence of network television, to magazine fare styled for the lip readers, to social contact with people so curiously predictable in their attitudes you know their lines before they say them.

Amid all my periods of this self-imposed diet of off-duty pabulum there has been the bright boon of cat watching, of communicating with these supra-pragmatic entities on an honorable level of cause and effect, of seeing both the jungly graces and the owlish slapstick. It has been the one form of intensive observation and conjecture so little related to the desk hours that it has freshened and restored.

Roger, in the exercise of his single feat of obedience to command, has never failed to cheer me. Long ago, when he hovered too close, within biting range, I would put a bare foot against his shoulder, and, saying "Down!" in a loud voice, I would shove him rudely over onto his side. In time it became simplified. If I made a threatening gesture with the foot and shouted the word, down he would go.

Now the word alone suffices, but he so hates to comply, it is an absurd and lengthy process. I yell the word at the cat. He is certain I cannot possibly mean it. He starts to walk away. I move to block his escape. "Down! Down! Down, you son of a gun!"

Perhaps I will be satisfied with less. He makes a small circle, walking with all knees bent. He looks up. This is enough? "Down!" He crouches against the floor. Certainly *this* is enough! "Down!" With a look of being at the weary end of his patience, he dips one shoulder and flops over onto his side. I pat the cat. After total surrender, he seems mightily pleased with himself. We understand each other and all the rules of the contest.

THIRTEEN

———◆———

The summer of 1957 was the last time we shipped the cats to Utica. They were in fine shape when we expressed them. They arrived at Dr. Sellman's in horrid condition after four days in transit. It was cold throughout the East, and he said that it seemed possible that somewhere along the line they had been left out of doors, perhaps on a station platform. The once legible statements of care given them en route had deteriorated to an indifferent, incomplete, indecipherable scrawl while, over the interim the cost had more than tripled.

The cats were eleven and twelve, too old to adjust readily to hardship and exposure, and certainly we did not feel right about risking them again to such slovenliness and indifference. Geoff wasn't badly off, but Roger was dangerously ill. We discussed it with Dr. Sellman. I had learned during Geoff's serious illness how to give a cat a pill. With thumb and forefinger on exactly the right place, the jaws will open. Then, using a dart-throwing motion, you throw the pill down into the upturned mouth, aiming at one side of the back of the tongue. Still keeping the mouth aimed upward, you close the jaws and hold them closed, and the cat's throat will work as he swallows. Geoff, aside from some devious business of pretending it was gone and spitting it out later, had been very good about it. But I had qualms about Roger. Nevertheless, we all agreed that a cat so sick had a better chance of recovery in a familiar place with his own people. They readily become depressed while in kennels.

So after the doctor treated him again, we wrapped him up warmly, and Dorothy held him in her lap while we drove them up to the lake. Once there it soon became evident that giving him his pills was no problem. He became weaker and weaker, until he could hardly lift his head. He was too weak to eat. We kept him in a box near the floor furnace. Dorothy was up every night several times, spooning warm milk into him. He was a few bones and sinews in a disreputable gray sack. After a time he stopped feeling as hot, and he did seem a little more responsive, but he was still terribly weak.

Even after seven years, Dorothy still recalls his moment of recovery with a certain amount of amused indignation. One afternoon was warm and sunny. She thought it might make him feel better if she carried his box out into the sunshine for a little while. She could watch him out the kitchen window.

Suddenly she looked out and saw the slat-sided cat get out of the box and wobble off in the direction of the clearing at the side of the house. Remembering the way Geoff had crept away to either recover or die, she hurried out. She found the old fool in the clearing, with painful slowness going through the unmistakable motions of the hunt. He looked at her with his idiot grin. In view of his hunting abilities when in peak condition, it was an incredibly optimistic performance.

Thereafter he recovered so quickly that in a couple of days it was a gory chore trying to get a pill down him. His new-found benignity stopped short of having his jaws pried open.

140

In the autumn we risked one final railroad trip. The weather was good. Again it took too long, and that was the time the inside of their box was such a fetid horror Geoff went immediately over and stood with his face in the hedge. I put the crate in the bay weighted down and let the tide cleanse it. After it was recovered and was dried out, I put it on the burning pile.

In June of 1958 Johnny graduated from Oakwood, and his application to work that summer in Mexico with the Friends Service Committee was approved. Though it seemed to him an instance of overprotectiveness, making him somewhat surly on the way down, we decided to drive him to Mexico, turn him over to the Quakers in Mexico City, and continue on down to Cuernavaca and spend the summer there after an absence of ten years. As it turned out, it was a good thing we went. Despite the required typhoid series, he acquired a galloping good case of typhoid out in the remote village where they were digging cisterns, a case that made us commuters to Mexico City, visiting him in the hospital there during his extended stay. It was severe enough to leave him with a permanently unreliable digestive system, and was especially alarming to Dorothy because her father had died of the same disease when she was fourteen.

In looking for a place to stow the cats in the summer of '58, someone told us about the Buckelwood Boarding Kennels off in the piney flatlands five or six miles southeast of Bradenton. It is owned by a Mr. and Mrs. Buchanan, a Quaker couple who have a great affection for animals and the competence to keep animals happy and healthy.

I must say that in Quaker hands the cats fared better than the boy that year. When we picked them up they were fat, smug, and glossy and had so firmly established themselves with the management that the Buchanans seemed a bit dubious about entrusting them to us. In fact, ever since we started that relationship, we have had the feeling that we are, in some subtle manner, borrowing the Buchanan cats while we are in Florida.

We boarded both cats with them in 1959 and 1960.

In the spring of 1960 Geoffrey began to act strangely. He was fourteen years old. Dorothy noted that he was not eating well. And he began to spend a great deal of time under a particular chair. He would spend very little time away from it and always go right back. He would beg for food when there was food in his dish, using that extremely effective nasty yap he had developed over the years. She would tempt him with the things he had always been fond of, and he would eat a very little bit and go back under the chair. Often he would keep turning this way and that, as though trying to find some position comfortable to him. As the weather grew warmer, he would sometimes move out onto the terrace under the shade of a bush and then return to his place under the chair. He seemed to like attention, and, remembering the third eyelid, we gave him a lot of it.

Each time when he seemed to be getting to the point where we should take him over to Dr. Thomas, he would improve. But he had gotten so thin he had lost that square look, and his coat, instead of lying flat and glossy, was tufted and dry-looking. He did not feel hot. His nose did not run. He did not seem to have diarrhea or any significant amount of vomiting. And he purred often. It is hard to judge what might have been the best decision.

Even more than Roger, he loathed the car and visits to the hospital. We hated to cause him discomfort when he apparently was in no pain other than the discomfort of getting up after staying too long in one position. We had taken him to Dr. Thomas when he first began to act sluggish. He had been given a vitamin shot. There was no other evident problem.

In the cat-to-human ratio of years, he was ninety-eight. Possibly the heat was bothering him. Now we both know we should have taken him to Dr. Thomas, but there is hardly anything in this life which could not be improved by hindsight.

When it came time to leave him at Buckelwood, he was having one of his better periods. We did not feel entirely easy about him, but he did seem well enough to leave, and we knew we could give him no better care than they would. We explained how he had been acting and we certainly did not expect him to die, or we would not have left him.

At Piseco we received this letter from Mrs. Buchanan:

BUCKELWOOD KENNELS REG.
Wm. and Frances Buchanan, Owners-Managers
Route 3, Manatee, Fla.

Aug. 4, 1960

Dear Mr. and Mrs. MacDonald,

I wish I didn't have to write this letter. I should have done it last night but I was so weary and I couldn't find words to say that we lost Geoffrey. He was gone when I went over at midnight to give him his Terramycin. We got it from a vet here in Bradenton and for a while it sure looked like he was going to make it. He was starting to eat again since my first letter. We had him on Terramycin every six hours and he was eating raw beef ground twice and chicken livers. His elimination had improved and we had separated him from Roger just putting him in the next cage but we put them together after he started eating again and Geoffrey could walk around.

On the first of Aug. I couldn't get him to touch anything except the chicken liver and then that came up also his medicine but then at 6 P.M. he retained his medicine but was so weak and he couldn't eat anything and acted like he didn't know me or anybody. At midnight when I went to check him he was gone.

After he was gone he wasn't flat like he should have been but his stomach was large and hard like there was a growth or sponge under the skin. He never seemed to be in any pain and wanted to be petted and loved up to the night before he died when he acted like he didn't know me.

Dr. Thomas called today and said that he didn't think anything could have been done for him, but to please tell you that he had called.

It has been so very hot here and when he was eating I didn't want to do anything to upset him again like carrying him all the way to Dr. Thomas in the heat and he just went so quick when he did stop again I didn't have a chance.

Roger is doing fine— His eye seems to hurt him some and keeps watering so we got some medicine for that now. He doesn't seem to miss Geoffrey so much it will be when he gets

143

home again that he will be looking for him. I wish I didn't have to write this letter. We didn't have much chance but we tried everything we knew.

We put Geoffrey in a wooden box and marked the grave so if you would like to take him back to Siesta Key when you come south again we can try to move the box. (He is under an orange tree on a little hill.)

He was a gentleman always so sweet and gentle and always so patient. When he was feeling good he still never cried at feeding time or scratched at his door like so many other cats do. He would always wait his turn and since he always had a choice of two or more things he ate what he liked best usually kidney and left the rest until later. He was so sweet it just doesn't seem possible he is gone.

I hope you can read this—some of it as I read it over again doesn't make much sense.

Sincerely yours
Frances Buchanan and Roger.

Dr. Thomas sent us a nice note also.

Certainly one weeps for a cat, as for any good thing spanning so many good years of a family. Especially vivid and sad to me is what happened about the third evening after we heard about him. I wandered out into the kitchen. Dorothy was fixing dinner. What happened needs a certain amount of background. In Dorothy's childhood her family was close and physically demonstrative. In the Scots household of my youth, I was on a handshake basis with my father at tender years. Physical habits condition the human animal. The buddy-boy male who drapes a hearty arm across my shoulders gives me the squirms. And though I have tried very hard to loosen up, and think sometimes I have achieved a fair imitation, Dorothy can detect in response to the casual affection of pat or squeeze, a woodenness consonant with a dour heritage.

Johnny was in the Greek islands that summer. Old Rog, despite mellowness, would set up a patient agitation to be put down whenever he was picked up, the change being that he would try to fumble free rather than rip his way clear.

I went into the kitchen, and Dorothy sniffed, and I knew it was about Geoff again. I tried for a comforting word, and she turned with wet eyes and edge-of-sobs expression and said with a tremulous dismay, "Now I'll have nothing left to hug."

As I did not want the Buchanans to think we blamed them in any way, I wrote them this letter:

8 August 1960

Dear Mrs. Buchanan,

We got your letter about Geoff in this afternoon's mail, and we have been grieved and depressed ever since, and will be for some time to come. He was a significant part of our household for over fourteen years, and we will miss him very much.

We know you did everything and more than anyone could expect, and we truly appreciate it all, as well as the concern, detail and understanding in your letter. As long as it had to happen we do wish he could have been at home with us when it did, but otherwise we're glad it happened there, where he was known and appreciated.

We do not yet know what we will wish to do, if anything, about moving him. We shall leave that up to our son. We are sending him your letter. In the very limited sense that one can "own" a cat, Geoff belonged to Johnny, and Roger is mine.

We know you feel badly that this should have happened. We have been telling each other that he had a very long and successful career and died with his awareness of being treated with love and respect intact.

We shall, of course, wonder how Rog adjusts to this emptiness in his familiar environment, and we would very much appreciate it if you could drop us a note a little later and tell us how he is acting.

Sincerely

We do not know what killed him. Elderly cats seem subject to malignancies of the liver. We do have one ironic suspicion. Some years earlier we had decided the Florida routine of the regular visit from the spray man who goes about the house fizzing his bug juice into the corners and cracks is not only overly costly but moderately ineffectual. And so we had arranged to have the house sprayed with deadlier chemicals while we were gone in the summer.

We remember that when we came back from Piseco in the autumn of '59 the job seemed most effective. It had had a good chance to air out, but there was enough residual effect to fell newcomers in their tracks.

Both cats frequently slept on the floor. Geoff did the washing for the two of them. It is just possible that by early 1960 Geoff had licked enough poison off the two of them to sicken him. And, of course, each time he began to feel a little better, he would go back to the washing chore and ingest more of it. It is only a guess.

FOURTEEN

When we picked Roger up at Buckelwood and took him home in the fall of 1960, we expected him to search for Geoff once back in familiar surroundings. But, of course, he'd had a cage to himself at Buckelwood after Geoff died. Always, except in case of illness, we requested that they be kept in the same cell.

Roger was delighted to be home. And he seemed equally delighted to be the only cat. All food, service, and sleeping places were his alone. He seemed to understand there was no other cat there and no point in looking for one. But once in a while, not oftener than once a week, we would hear him, usually out in the screened cage, making that a-rowr? a-rowr? which was forever the call to game-time.

Deprived of the customary rough-and-tumble he perfected the substitute which he had begun to devise during the previous spring when Geoff would not play. Perhaps because of the malformed feet, Roger makes an astonishing amount of noise on a hardwood floor when he runs. It is a ba-rumm, ba-rumm, ba-rumm sound, exactly like the hoof rhythm of a galloping horse. Thus the name of the game became the Flying Red Horse, a dead giveaway as to the age of certain parties who used to hear it on a radio commercial long ago. It would usually begin out in the screened terrace and still does. It is a morning game, most probably when the people are on the second cup of coffee. Having the doors open to the living room and to the studio in warm weather enhances the game. First there is the arched back, the tail slightly puffed, a feisty little sidelong scamper, as though he is avoiding some opponent visible only to him. Then there are some yammerings, and he breaks into his gallop. Some days it takes up the stairs to my work area and back down again, but always through the studio and kitchen, around and around, hoofs drumming, ears laid back. There is always at least one reckless transit under the couch, this accomplished by stretching out on the back and using the claws to dig into the underside of the low couch and pull himself along at a good pace. It always ends with his scrambling recklessly up onto the long bar, using chair back and stools to get there, running the length of the bar, then, panting, mouth open, looking terribly fierce, he reaches his claws as high as he can on the four-by-four post at the end of the bar.

I suspect that this is a rare activity for an old party of 130. Reflexes and elasticity being not what they were, he sometimes miscalculates. Twice this past season he has misjudged the leap to the bar, scrabbled at it, slipped, fallen. The game ends there. The humiliated cat walks away.

When the game is successfully concluded, wild passion spent, he finds himself atop the bar. He *can* get down, but it is a jolt to old bones and muscles he would rather avoid if possible, and cons the people into lifting him down. Not long ago, in the middle of the night, I awoke and heard him, all alone in the dark house, being a Flying Red Horse. I cannot say why it seemed so touching.

In the fall of 1960 we depressed him by bringing a bird home. It was a male meadow lark which had been clipped by a car. Dorothy stopped and picked it up from the shoulder of the road. When we got it settled down, it showed no signs of being able to recover and fly away. When it walked, it walked in a small, tight circle, right through its water dish if it happened to be in the way. When it tried to fly it put one wing tip down and flapped in an equally small circle. We put it on the terrace and closed the doors so Roger could not get at it. It did not have sufficient co-ordination to eat, so Dorothy mixed up some suitable goo, and we fed it with an eye dropper. Roger could not understand why he was being denied the terrace, why we were keeping a bird, why he was not permitted to eat said bird. He would stare out at it and moan and drool visibly. He could taste it.

It began to co-ordinate a little better, but if it tried to hurry it ran in a circle, and if it tried to fly it tipped to one side. A young brain surgeon visiting on the Point said it had a brain clot which might or might not become reabsorbed. The trouble was food. They eat bugs. And it was that rare time of year in Florida when bugs are hard to find. We'd leave on the front-porch floodlight for hours and get perhaps two medium moths, enough to last a meadow lark one fraction of a second. I thought of fried grasshoppers and went over to The Beach Shop at Stickney Point Road and bought a can from George Connaly. They were a success. They had been caught and fried in Japan and shipped halfway around the world, and that meadow lark had to rekill each one, pick it up, slam it down onto the stone floor, peck at it, knock it around, chase it, and eat it.

The bird began to make longer flights and seemed to land where he intended to land. Finally we wedged the outside screen door open and herded him out. He stood on the little porch, stood on one foot and then the other, and then zoomed up over the punk trees and away. Roger, given access once more to the terrace, spent a long long time tiptoeing around, quivering, pointing like a bird dog, looking behind every leaf for that tasty bird.

Johnny came home, awaiting acceptance to a new term at Cranbrook Academy of Art in Michigan. We had all noticed a strange thing about Roger. He would be walking across the room, and all of a sudden he would stop and lie down on his belly and put a forearm across his eyes and stay there motionless, often for over an hour. When he got up again he would seem shaky, and he would avoid the light, very much like a human recovering from a blinding headache. It did not seem to affect his morale otherwise, but quite obviously the animal was in pain during those periods. The bad eye had been opaque for some time, and now it looked bulged to us. The intervals of pain were becoming more frequent.

It was Johnny who suggested we find out if it should come out. We took him over to Dr. Thomas, who examined him and said that the eye should certainly be removed; we could leave him right there, and he would do it. The bad eye had developed glaucoma and was badly distended. Though I certainly had every reason to feel confidence in the gentleman's ability, I hemmed and hawed and asked him, clumsily, if he . . . ah . . . did very much of this sort of . . . uh . . . thing. He said, with both reassurance and a slight indignation, that he had taken a refresher course in animal ophthalmology just that past summer.

We got Roger the next day. The eye had been removed and the furry lids sewn together, implausibly, with bright green thread. He was a very groggy cat. The general anesthetic made his rear end slump to one side or the other when he tried to walk. If I had to describe his attitude with just one word, I would say he acted thoughtful. The doctor had confirmed the idea the cat had been in severe pain.

We had to take him back several times for treatment. I cannot imagine a treatment a cat would find any more unpleasant. Behind the sutured lids the empty socket fills with fluid. The doctor has to pick open a small vent between the stitches to let the serum escape, and press as much out as he can.

Roger's response was as fantastic as anything I ever hope to see. He had always despised automobiles, always mourned with every breath he drew. By the time we took him back all effects of the anesthetic had worn off. He had demonstrated at home that he was not at all groggy. And that cat sat upright on the seat between us all the way over, ears forward in that catlook of eagerness, making not a sound of complaint. And he was visibly glad to arrive there, purring as he was carried in.

He hollered at the treatment, but he did not get frantic, and his struggles were brief and not overly violent. And he was amiable all the way home.

The next visit a few days later was exactly the same, except that he sat on the treatment table and needed only Johnny's hand on his shoulders to restrain him. When Dr. Thomas hurt the eye, Roger would yipe and flinch back, seem to gather himself, and then crane forward again, tilting his head, presenting the wound to the surgeon.

There can be only the one plausible explanation that the cat made a rational adjustment to cause and effect. The eye had been giving him constant pain which at times became much worse. He was taken to a place. The pain stopped. So he associated the place with the cessation of pain.

As it healed, as suppuration ceased, the sealed lids sank back to form a little furry pocket. We were supposed to take him to have the stitches removed, but Roger with a hideous and savage delicacy, removed them with one rear toenail, doing himself no harm. We got to him to stop him just as he was removing the last one.

It did bother us to look at him. Then suddenly it bothered us no more. When people see him for the first time, I often surprise a little expression of queasiness, and I have to quell my indignation by remembering how we, too, found it disturbing at first. In his best days he had that turtlehead, the high rear end, the bowed front legs, the unwashed gray of all the feet. Now the tail is shorter, an ear is ragged, the eye is gone, the front legs more bowed, the high rear end narrower, the loose underbelly swinging as he walks. And we find him exceptionally beautiful. Dorothy tells him this frequently.

He was our solitary boarder at Buckelwood the summer of 1961. Having had one of them die, the Buchanans were afraid they might lose the other one. And having the eye gone did not make him look sturdier. When we picked him up in the fall, Mrs. Buchanan confessed that when we had left him off she had the feeling he wouldn't make it.

We had some other cats at the lake the next summer for a little while. Johnny was by then married to his Anne, and when they stayed with us at Piseco en route to Nova Scotia, where her parents, Brinton and Mary Colfelt, have a summer residence, they brought along two cats they had been writing us about—Jaymie, a gray tiger adolescent cat, and Grey, a kitten, a soft blue-gray like summer smoke. Jaymie was a fine cat, responsive, fabulously healthy, crouching and dashing amid the Piseco rocks, the alder and scrub maple, the tall dark woods, playing the game of savage beast at the dawn of time, racing back to the people from time to time for approval and reassurance. Grey, still small enough to be mostly anonymous kitten, was showing the first personality traits of a kind of Rogerism, skeptical, slightly surly, intractable in the face of any kind of persuasion.

When summer ended and they went back to Michigan, to Cranbrook Academy of Art at Bloomfield Hills, where Johnny and Anne were to get a bachelor's and master's respectively, the following June, they rented a little frame farmhouse on seventy-eight acres of land, about a forty-minute drive from the school.

When we got back to Sarasota in the fall of 1962, we got our elderly party out of his summer resort. He was glossy and solid and in good spirits, but the Buchanans reported that he was drinking an extraordinary amount of water, and they did not like the way the remaining eye would sometimes catch and reflect the light.

We observed him carefully as he settled into his Point Crisp routine. He certainly was drinking a great deal of water, and the toilet in the east bathroom was his water hole. He did not want water which had been sitting there quietly for any length of time, nor the water in his water dish. He wanted it fresh-flushed, and quickly learned how to con both of us, so that whoever was nearest would flush it for him. He would get up onto the seat and circle it until he was at that position where he could step down with his front feet onto the porcelain slope above the water level. Prior to that winter it had been an infrequent occurrence to see that high, scrawny back end sticking up out of the plumbing, but in the winter of 1962–63 it was a standard scene.

We could not detect any sign of ill health. His nose was a hearty pink. His coat was glossy. He was a Flying Red Horse from time to time. He bit. He adored. He yaffled. He appeared, sometimes, for the sock game. He flopped onto his side on command, after the usual reluctance and half measures. He went calling. We both imagine that this water-hunger has been an adjustment to one of the customary degenerative diseases of ancient cats. Heathcliffe, before he had to be killed by the vet, had a great deal of kidney and bladder trouble and became sporadically more incontinent. Roger apparently keeps his water system in top shape by overworking it.

We watched that eye. It did not have the milky look we remembered as the first sign of trouble in the other eye. But when the light would catch it just right there would be, for an instant, a slight opacity. I suspect, and there would seem to be no good way to check it, that there are just enough dead cells in the eye fluid to create this effect under the right conditions. We have many birds on the Point, from the wading yellow-eyed fish-stalkers to the smallest warblers. And old Rog, from inside the house, will at times look through the glass doors, through the terrace screening, between the branches of the fringe of water oaks, and cat-watch an immature heron on a little oyster bar a hundred feet off our back shore, his ears slanted forward, body very slightly crouched and motionless, tail tip flickering. It takes us so long to spot what is interesting him that we do not worry about the efficiency of that eye. If it is slowly fading, it is at a rate which will make it last longer than the rest of him.

That fall his increasing deafness became more noticeable. He seemed to hear me more readily than he could hear Dorothy, so we can assume that he was losing the higher cps range. When he slept in one position too long, it seemed difficult for him to get up and loosen old muscles. Dr. Thomas recommended the occasional shot of cortisone. It limbers him nicely and, to our surprise, improves his hearing for several weeks after he has a shot. When we have to be away for just a few days it is simpler to board him with Dr. Thomas than way off at Buckel-wood, and so when we leave him there now, we ask for the cortisone shot as a matter of course.

That was the winter he gave up going out at night. It was his decision. He would ask to go out. Someone would hold the screen door open for him. He would stop halfway out and apparently try to use his nose, his eyesight, his hearing, to check the blackness out there. I suspect that it was being unable to hear anything, which made the night more fearful to him. Silence can be something waiting. He would think it over, back into the house and wheel around, and plod out through the kitchen to the studio and from there out through the door we left wedged open for him onto the screened terrace. Incidentally, it took both cats two or three seasons to become absolutely convinced the terrace was entirely enclosed and that nothing could get at them out there. The birds using the feeder just beyond the screen were quicker, apparently, to comprehend that cats could not get out.

Yet this is an area where it is often erroneous to attempt to gauge the extent of comprehension of a cat. Observation is a faulty tool in the face of a cat's apparent delight in frightening itself. It seems to be one of those functional games to keep the adrenalin perked up. When a visiting dog has been prowling around the house, snuffling his way past the terrace, we have seen Geoff give every evidence of wanting to get out there through the screen and teach that dog what for, apparently saying, "Boy, if I could just get out there . . ."

Then a day or so later, when he would see something he thought he might be able to catch, there was no problem. He would freeze, stare at it, then whirl and go through the studio, kitchen, living room, hallway, into the dressing room, and out his window in a low, silent run.

As they seemed to play these games of terror and pretend, they also had a very shrewd judgment when it came to actual danger as opposed to bluff. One time Mary, Dorothy's first cousin, came to Piseco with her husband, Eugene Hubbard, a Utica attorney, and their dachshund, named Fritz. Fritz was visibly appalled at the size of the resident cats. But when he discovered they planned to politely ignore him, he made a serious miscalculation and tried to push his luck. He began to trot around with ever increasing jauntiness and began to yap at them. He confused tolerance with timidity. When he began to get on their nerves, one of them waited for him just around a corner of the house, and when he came trotting around the corner, a horror was standing there, inches away, a cat standing so tall and haired up it was the size of a bushel basket. It showed long white fangs, satanic green eyes, and made a sound like a broken steam valve. Fritz went plunging and yodeling through the woods and ran all the way out the length of our eighty-foot dock, a narrow structure on sunken sawhorses, and cowered at the far end, screaming about what he had seen. The cats had made not the slightest attempt to follow him. They came strolling onto the dock in front where the people were, lounged about, and began buffing their fingernails on their lapels and whistling tunelessly. Fritz had to be carried to the safety of their car and enclosed there before he ceased moaning and muttering.

However, one day while the guesthouse was being built, the young architect who had designed it came to check on the work, bringing in his convertible his big, rangy cat-killing black poodle. When he brought the dog he would put a leash on it and leave it tethered inside the car. That day as he reached to snap the leash on it, the dog spotted Roger in the side yard. It vaulted out of the car and went after Roger in deadly and purposeful silence. The cat-killers waste no time barking and circling. When he had been interested in the osprey, Roger had found an intricate way to climb up to the garage roof. When the poodle came at him he went up there again, but not the same way. He went right up the side of the house, and we cannot understand how he managed it, and he might never have been able to do it again, but it saved his life.

During their Christmas holidays, Johnny and Anne drove to Florida, bringing Jaymie and Grey. Jaymie was the compleat cat, and Grey was the adolescent. The size and the look of Roger alarmed them. Grey, at Roger's delicate, inquisitive, placating approach, backed swiftly under a couch and made a noise unlike any they had yet heard him make. Except for his permanent feud with Heathcliffe, Roger has never made objection to other cats in the house. With small cats there is a reversion to that maternal urge. And he wants to play with the larger ones. While they are still uneasy about him, he will pounce elaborately upon some long-ignored catnip mouse and bat it about as they watch him, as if he were trying to demonstrate his innocent intent.

They became accustomed to him, and the three cats romped, but Roger could not keep up the pace. About five frantic minutes would do him in and he would leave the game and go get some rest. And, in action, they were a little too speedy and agile for him, so that he wound up often cuffing at the empty place where a cat had just been.

He enjoyed having them around. Johnny, Anne, and the cats lived in the guesthouse. The cat window was returned to service. In the dressing room there is a small, low chest of drawers. The top of it is eight or nine inches below the window sill, just the right height for Roger to sit on the chest with his forearms resting on the sill while he stares out at the night through the hole cut in the screen.

Night after night after the visiting cats were gone, we would wonder where Roger was and go look for him and find him sitting in the dressing room in the dark, an absurd and touching sight from behind, like a tired woman at a tenement window looking out at the street. He did not want to go out into that darkness, but he sat there waiting for those other cats and looking for them.

Here are some passages from a letter Johnny wrote us the following April (written on a Saturday after Jaymie had been gone since the previous Monday):

"We have looked and called and combed the roadsides, but he blended into the grass so well we could step right over him without seeing. We have gone through many theories and only one seems to fit. Two weeks ago we heard real wildcats screaming behind the house. We think nine pound Jaymie could cope with anything that moved except a forty pound Jaymie . . . He died at night, not by human agency of car or gun, but in his own world; so, as our friend Tullio said, 'He may have been beaten, but he wasn't confused.' . . . Anne is up to her nose in degree furies. I am simply waiting for James."

FIFTEEN

———◆———

Johnny and Anne had acquired other livestock that spring
—rabbits, some ducks, a pair of goslings. The geese
adopted them as parents. By the time the geese were half
grown, Johnny and Anne had become so enchanted with
their responsiveness, intelligence, fastidiousness, and the
ducks, by comparison, seemed such mindless, offensive,
noisy, sloppy gluttons, they began to dine on duck.

Geese are fantastically effective watchdogs. In the middle of one night there was a horrible racket out back. By
then the wildcats had cleaned out most of the small creatures in their wood lot. That night they or it came to eat
goose. They slew the gander and opened a long gash in the
neck of the goose, before the kids were able to get out
there and drive it away. Johnny and Anne had named the
female Knees, a name which will seem apt to anyone who
has stared with any objectivity at the knees of a goose. She
was understandably agitated, and they brought her into
the house, bandaged her neck, finally got her settled down.

When they took walks, Knees and Grey would accompany them. Geese are not constructed for walks in the woods. They cannot see where they are stepping. She would do the best she could and wait noisily to be picked up and hoisted over obstacles she couldn't manage. There were references to Knees in every letter. We felt that a goose could be nothing other than a rather absurd-looking idiot.

They wrote us of leaving Knees alone outside one day when they went on an errand. When they came back she was gone. As they were looking for her, the phone rang. A farmer nearly a half mile down the highway had her, and they drove down to find the farmer and his wife and Knees standing on the porch. Knees acted nervous and gave them elaborate greetings.

The farmer said that he had seen this here white goose going across that back lot out there, flat out, wings spread, running like hell, apparently with something chasing it. Thinking he might scare off whatever was after it, he had given a yell, whereupon Knees had spotted him, veered, and come directly to him to stand and lean against his leg, staring out into the field and talking a blue streak. Considerably rattled, he had headed back to the house with the goose practically underfoot, talking every step of the way. There it had climbed the steps to the porch, and damn if it didn't act as if it knew they were going to come after it.

Knees and Grey were at the camp when we got there last summer. Johnny and Anne had arrived first and opened it up.

There is room for Knees in this cat book, because this book is concerned with how living creatures display their separate personalities only when there is trust and security and, most of all, attention.

She was almost full-grown when she first saw water she could swim in. She went into it at once and headed off until she was a tiny white spot. At first she was a bad swimmer. She couldn't stroke properly. Each thrust would swing her tail over toward the side opposite the thrust, so that instead of gliding she wobbled from side to side. When Anne went down to the dock and called her, Knees

160

came heading back from far away, giving a resounding, triumphant QUONK every fifty feet.

That first night she spent a happy hour in front of the floodlight by the deck, snapping moths out of the air with that multi-purpose beak. The kids were planning a trip very soon and were testing a tent they had erected under the pine trees back of the camp. When they went off to bed, they called Knees, and she went waddling along with them, keeping up a continuous conversation.

In a few days they left, taking Grey, leaving Knees with us. By then Knees had given us her approval. We knew the formula for goose soup—cylindrical duck pellets which dissolve in water to make a greenish and singularly nasty-looking mess. Just as she was more responsive to Anne than to Johnny, she was more responsive to Dorothy than to me.

We were most astonished by the "vocabulary" she had. There was a greeting noise, made when you approached her. This was accompanied by a series of low bows, strangely oriental in flavor. There was the eating noise when she was presented with soup, an ecstatic and delighted little chuckling that she could continue to make even when her bill was deep in the soup. She liked the soup donor to stay close by, preferably sitting on his or her heels on the other side of the bowl. Knees would stop the chuckling and soup-sucking at regular intervals to lift her head high and stare directly and fixedly into your face. For some reason a goose, head on, staring at you, looks cross-eyed.

There was quiet conversation—when adult was inert and goose was paddling about or trudging about, a kind of peaceful little quabbling sound. There was excited conversation, such as when she was going for a walk, a swim, or a boat ride. This was a quabbling carried on at a louder and faster rate, punctuated every little while by one or two of those huge, resonant QUONK sounds. Sometimes QUANK!

After Dorothy found that Knees adored having fresh grass pulled for her, she developed a con-artist sound, a tiny, inquisitive, plaintive queeping, head tilted, leaning

161

hesitantly toward the thicket where the good grass grew, and which she dared not enter. Pull the poor little goose some grass.

There were the almost inaudible little peeps she made when composing herself for sleep. There were the huge series of trumpeted quonkings giving warning of anyone or anything coming by land or by sea—in the daylight.

There was the guttural little sound she made while preening and combing herself after the elaborate daily bath, a kind of expression of diligence and satisfaction.

It surprised us to learn that geese yawn and also snore.

The one kind of conversation which most intrigued us cannot be explained without discussing her daily routine. After the kids left she took over a small, shallow bay directly in front of the house. It lies to the left of the small, thickety peninsula leading to the dock. A spur of rock runs off to the left, making her bay into a U with the opening to the left, a U about ten feet across and ten feet long. Her dish was on the sand rim of the U opposite the opening.

Geese apparently have phenomenal eyesight and hearing. In the flock they must somehow have a rotating-duty system for the sentry geese. Being a one-goose flock is a very serious and exhausting business indeed. She was very white. She was such an impressive, blazing white that even by starlight we could see her out there standing on the end of the dock, no matter at what time of night we looked out, head very high, tense and alert and sleepless. We learned she seemed a lot more relaxed if we left the flood-lights turned on. They did not reach that far, but as least she seemed to feel she could see anything that might be coming after her from the bushes.

In the daytime if you called to her, you would get the big, jolly QUANK routine. If you called to her at night, you would get an answer you could just barely hear. And so we fell into the habit of going down there each night to say good night to the goose. Her conversation was hilarious. It was a variation of the daytime excited gabbling, but it was carried on in such a hushed tone, it was exactly like a person whispering. She would keep turning her head from side to side, inspecting the darknesses about, and she was obviously telling us of all the horrors lurking about. It was such a convincing performance we would find ourselves talking very quietly too. One night she got so carried away with her recital of terrors, she gave out with one great, shocking, rusty QUONK that frightened her into an abrupt silence. She listened for a long time, then began muttering to us again.

One night we saw her down there floating in her little bay. We spoke, and there was absolutely no response. We went down to the water's edge. Still without a sound she came out of the water and paddled around behind me and stood leaning against me and looking out around my leg. Only then did she make the faintest of sounds, and it seemed like controlled hysteria. She could not have said, more clearly, "It's really after me tonight." She came back up to the house with us, glancing back, talking more bravely. I lifted her onto the deck. She went at once to the screen door to be let in. We let her in with certain reluctance. The venerable expression—loose as a goose—is soundly anchored to reality. But we couldn't leave her out there. We piled furniture to keep her sequestered in the kitchen and bedroom hallway area and paved it with newspapers. Once inside she talked ever more loudly. When she began to settle down we went to bed, leaving our bedroom door wedged open about three inches so we could hear her if she got tangled up in anything out there. In bed, we heard her come flapping along the hall, muttering. She stuck her head through the three-inch gap, extended the full length of her long white neck, gave one huge, jolly, ear-shattering QUANK, and then padded back to the kitchen. That night we heard a wildcat scream.

We were afraid a precedent had been set, but that was the only night all summer long she demanded refuge. I don't think she was kidding.

In daytime excited talk she loved to have Dorothy quabble back at her, and she would put that bill an inch from Dorothy's lips, and they would go it at a great rate, Knees getting more and more agitated.

She did a lot of sleeping each morning, from first light on, catching up from the night's vigil, standing on one ridiculous foot, head laid along her back. By midmorning she was hearty and cheerful. Because of a large and very shallow rocky shelf about 150 feet off our shore, I mark it with a buoy each summer to keep water skiers from bursting their primitive skulls upon it, and as a guide to friends visiting in their boats. The buoy is round, larger than a basketball, and floats high, painted half red and half white, the white side uppermost as it floats. Day after day, Knees would swim out particularly when the lake had a slight chop, and float right beside that buoy, bobbing up and down with it. I imagine that, driven by the flock instinct, it was the nearest thing to another goose she could find.

The daily ablution, performed in her little bay, was extensive. She would dip her head in a manner that would lift water up and send it running down her back, pausing to dig at herself, ruffle herself up, send small feathers drifting downwind. After at least ten minutes of this, she would do surface dives and swim underwater, going outside her bay and swimming ten and fifteen feet at a time, visible from the dock as a swift, white, and very graceful shape. If, as Anne discovered, people would gather around, clap their hands, and say Good Goose, she could be induced to keep the underwater act up for much longer than usual. After this portion of the routine, she would stand at the end of the rock ridge and preen herself for a half hour. There are oil glands under their wings, and these secretions are used to smooth down each feather. Twice in the summer some motorboat oil drifted in, giving her a ring like a nasty bathtub. Each time she just kept washing over and over until it was gone, hour after hour of effort.

The first time the merganser family came along, Knees became terribly excited. She went after them, big white wings flapping, big web feet running along the surface of the water, neck outstretched, honking enthusiastic greetings. At this apparition, the ducks took off like rockets. She sat on the water and watched them go and paddled back to her bay. After that, she never paid the slightest bit of attention to them. She gave no evidence of hearing them or seeing them even when they passed within ten feet of the end of the dock.

No one in the family could go out in a boat without Knees insisting on coming along. Rowboat, kicker boat, canoe, sailboat, her self-assigned place was in the bow, standing tall, honking at everything in sight. Dorothy has a water bicycle at the lake which she uses during the last of the daylight. When she took it out, Knees would come paddling along, hollering. Dorothy would stop; Knees would flounder up onto one of the aluminum pontoons, and off they would go into the sunset. But on the water bike, Knees was usually very silent. She would make some *sotto voce* comments, watch the shore carefully, then manage to fall off as awkwardly as possible when they returned to the little bay.

People liked to either troll slowly for bass out beyond our rocks, or anchor and fish. Knees trumpeted at every passing boat. The very slow ones and the ones which anchored got her so excited she could not contain herself. Sooner or later she would take off in that dead run, that half-flying, half-running zoom across the top of the water right at the boat. Reaching it she would settle down and then merely circle it if it was anchored, or go along with it if it was trolling, quabbling loudly. The smart fishermen learned they either had to lift her into the boat or go fish somewhere else. Once in an early morning mist she went so far down the lake shore, escorting some fishermen, I could no longer see her or them from the dock. But I could hear her, and I could hear the plaintive voice of the fisherman overriding hers, pleading, "Go home, duck! For God's sake, go home!"

I saw one friendly approach which could have turned out disastrously for Knees. A boat was about a hundred yards out from our dock. A man and a woman were in it, fishing. Knees, after considerable racket, worked herself up to the proper pitch and took off. She could be quite a sight to an unsuspecting stranger, big white wings flapping, feet slapping the surface of the water, coming right at you, quonking furiously, moving at perhaps twenty miles an hour. While the man merely stared at the oncoming goose, the woman sprang to her feet, grabbed an oar and took aim like Mickey Mantle. Some people are afraid of birds, and some have heard that geese are dangerous, confusing them, no doubt, with swans. Knees halted ten feet short of the boat. The woman sat down. The man started the motor, and they roared away from there, and Knees came paddling thoughtfully home.

Usually, when boats did not leave, if we called to Knees she would often come chugging in, talking all the way about what she'd been doing.

When anybody went swimming, she was transported. She would go right along with them, yap into their faces, and try to stand on their shoulders. With Johnny and Anne, she would dive and circle their legs, brushing against them under water.

Best of all, Knees loved the catamaran. I had ordered it. It came in a cardboard box of suitable size to make a coffin for the Cardiff giant. The detailed instructions said the average twelve-year-old could put it together in an afternoon. It took me three days, plus considerable help the final afternoon from Dorothy's brother. Under sail, the people sit on a canvas sling, about eight feet square, not unlike a trampolin, laced to a frame elevated six inches above the twin hulls.

We had only to start rigging the sail, and Knees would come out of a sound sleep and come paddling around the headland toward the other bay, quonking with expectant pleasure.

Not long before Labor Day, Dorothy and I took Knees on her final sail of the summer. We crossed the lake and ran slowly before a light breeze down the row of camps on the other side, about sixty feet off shore. By then Knees was a celebrity bird all over that lake.

We would hear child voices yell from shore. "Hey! There's Knees! Hi, Knees. Hey, Knees!" And that bird would respond, each time, by gathering herself and giving out with such huge honks, they resonated and echoed off the hills and deafened us and delighted a whole lake shore of children.

Our nephew, John Prentiss, visited us one day last summer and brought Kristin to meet us, the girl he is now married to. Kristin has lovely long hair, a natural strawberry blond shade. They sat down by the dock, and Knees circled Kristin, gabbling with excited approval. And finally she began to preen Kristin's long hair, strand by strand, working her way around the girl's head, uncannily gentle, making her small pleasure sounds for the entire fifteen minutes it took.

I used the incident in a short story which *This Week* Magazine published in November 1963.

The goose was the good thing last summer, and Grey was the bad thing. He had grown into a large and handsome cat and, I am afraid, a bold and reckless cat. The second trip Johnny and Anne took, they left Grey with us too. He was happy and busy. He despised Knees, probably resenting the attention she got. When he learned how afraid she was of any subtle rustling in the brush, he would torment her in the evening by stalking her, sometimes sending her in a wild honking dash out to where she would float beside her buoy, reluctant to return.

It was his habit in the evening to go in and out through the window a half dozen times after dark, before we went to bed. One night he went out just before dark. He didn't return during the evening. We went out and called him. He did not return all night. Had he returned, he would have made himself evident. He had a curious trick. He didn't sleep with the people, but when he decided it was time they should get up, he didn't holler. He merely walked across them, stomping. He would step lightly at other times. In the early morning he would deliberately stomp. There is no other word to describe it.

For days we walked and searched and called. Had he been in the area and alive, he certainly could have found his way back by the periodic daytime QUONK of Miss Knees. Maybe something got him. Possibly, on the other hand, somebody picked him up. He was a handsome cat with a perfect confidence that all people bore him good will. He would have gone up to anyone who spoke to him.

It is a miserable experience to lose someone else's cat. Johnny and Anne were all too tolerant about it, though very saddened to lose him so soon after losing Jaymie. After all the years and all the cats, the odds ran out last summer.

SIXTEEN

They took Knees back to Michigan. She had made some casual attempts to build a nest in the grass near the Piseco dock. Back in Michigan, each night, they put her on a small screened porch. She built a nest at the foot of the porch steps at one side. One morning Anne found Knees running back and forth in front of the screen door in considerable agitation. It was a cold morning. Anne opened the door, Knees ran out, plumped herself into her grass nest and stood up moments later to reveal a large, steaming goose egg. One has eggs on the nest, not on the porch.

They came down to visit us last Christmas. They boarded Knees with a very sympathetic veterinary they know, and by Christmas they had replaced Jaymie and Grey with five cats and brought them all along.

I shall not go into the characters, habits, traumas, and inter-personal relationships of Lisa, Gimli, Abishag, and group, except to say that I would rather burn bamboo under my fingernails than drive three thousand miles with five cats.

It is too bad Roger was in sorry shape while they were there. The minor athletics of the water hole had become too much for him, and he had settled for a yellow water dish under the bathroom lavatory, which he kept conning one or the other of us to empty and refill with fresh. He slept a great deal, had difficulty getting onto his feet, walked like an old, old man, and was not interested in going outdoors even in the daytime. No Flying Red Horse. Meager appetite.

As far as appetite is concerned, Roger never hollered for his food. During Geoff's lifetime he never had to. Geoff hollered for two. After Geoff died, Roger's procedure was to go to his kitchen corner when Dorothy was getting a meal and merely sit and stare up at her with a total, fixed, placid expectancy. Every time she glanced down, he was looking into her face. Unlike Geoff and most other animals, Roger has never been reluctant to stare you right in the eye. And, if there is a face on his level, as when he is atop the bar, he likes to tuck his chin under, purr, and press his furry forehead against yours.

During this past year Roger has added one new little trick to a lifetime of improvisation. Dorothy almost always wears barefoot sandals. When she is at the sink and has not noticed him for what he considers too long a period, he moves closer to sit with one front paw resting on the top of her foot. It is a trusting and gentle reminder. Here is your cat. It is not something which could be an accident. It is too consistent. It establishes physical contact and, as such, is related to affection. For an old cat it seems that the food relationship becomes somewhat ceremonial, with a customary pattern of asking and receiving, even when it ends with but one small mouthful and the plodding return to the soft couch.

Though he was not well last Christmas, the welter of visiting cats stimulated him, and he tried to respond. The little ones were wary of him, and in choosing up sides for the games did not need him. Once, while they were there, he assayed a rather enfeebled rendition of Flying Red Horse, but unfortunately his route brought him face to face with a waspish female with a sore mouth named Lisa, and after an abrupt stop, he turned and walked away with what little dignity was left him.

After kids and cats had left, Roger became worse. I found I hated one thing most of all. I hated to go out into the living room in the morning and see him asleep there and be on his bad eye side, with him too deaf to know I was up. Sooner or later he would sense some presence, perhaps through the transmitted vibrations of my footsteps, and give a sudden start and snap his head around and stare, then give the curl-tongue morning yawn, the slow, careful stretchings, then the hesitant descent from the low couch to come over and bump a head against a leg and get a morning scuffle of neck hair and under the white chin. Cats are so vibrantly alert, it seems some manner of indecent cheating to be able to come up on one in such inadvertent secrecy.

We thought it was the end of him, the machine wearing down. It was depressing but inevitable.

We have a phonograph record we have played once or twice a year for many years. It is a musical designed just for the record—*archy and mehitabel* with Carol Channing. There is a part where archy has said good-by forever, and, after a long absence, one morning they find that, during the night, that little cockroach has come back and has started leaving messages in the office typewriter.

Roger came back, and we could accept it with the same surprise and joy as in Carol's voice at the return of archy. He didn't come back overnight, but it was swift. Once more the muddy paw prints on the toilet seat, the great, noisy galloping, the clownishness, the imaginary horrors, the office visits to inspect the cupboards, the daytime walks, the exquisitely sensuous reactions to being brushed, the unexpected bites, the paw reaching to grab at the passerby, the sock game, the distant bird observed, the disdainfully easy cowing of any visiting dog. In all the ways a cat can communicate, he keeps saying, "I feel good!"

The top of the back of a living-room couch is level with the sill of a picture window, forming a fine cat place, where he can loll and look benign and see everyone who comes.

A few weeks ago a woman stopped at the house. She was very intense about the cat. She did not use baby talk exactly, but with a very dramatic delivery, expressing pathos and tragic concern, she exclaimed, "Oh, the poor old *thing!* Oh, the *poor* old thing! Oh, the *poor, old, thing!*"

One could imagine, from her tone, that the next question would be why we didn't have him put out of his misery. It surprised me to find out how much that approach irritated and offended me. There was no way to tell her that Roger is not a tragic figure. No matter how he must look to the casual visitor, he is by his own terms and reactions, a gutsy broth of a boy, a scampering youth, a canny con artist—and, at the same time, a pillar of the only community he knows.

I owe a strange debt to both cats. We got them when I was trying to learn how to write. There were the fifteen years of Geoffrey, and, by this coming fall, nineteen years of Roger. With no intention of seeming intolerant, I would like to say that I do not believe the dependent adorations of dogs could have formed the same necessary kind of emotional counterpoint. The elegant complexity of cats, the very formality of their codes of behavior, their unbribed response of sporadic demonstrations of affection in return for their demanded measure of household equality, their conservative insistence on order, habit, and routine —these attributes seem more congruent with lengthy creative effort, more contributive to that frame of mind which makes such effort sustainable than could be any doggy devotion.

There is a morality equation involved also, which might be better left unstated, but I cannot resist attempting it. The theme has been, of course, that the animal—given trust, security, affection, attention—will respond in ways which demonstrate an individuality, a uniqueness, a reasoning power which otherwise would remain hidden behind that traditional unresponsive façade of the unaffiliated cat. The equation says that the continuous exercise of

172

the attitude which causes the cat to reveal himself is, in time, self-revelatory as well.

Roger is at Buckelwood. Dorothy and I came down here to hide away and get in a full month of intensive work. I drove him out to Buckelwood before we left. Mrs. Buchanan hugged him, and Roger looked triumphantly fatuous. Once in his high cage, he immediately checked the food dish and the water dish and settled down, narrowing his eye in the sleepy expression of the contented purr.

In June, Johnny and Anne will arrive with tribe of cats and move into the guesthouse until they find a place of their own. They, along with another couple, are opening a fine-arts press setup. We shall stay in Sarasota well into July to see them settled and organized before we leave for the camp in the Adirondacks.

We shall have a chance, before leaving, to see how well Roger, now in good health and spirits, fits into the cat tribe. If the adjustment is good, we shall leave him with them for the summer. But it well may be that though a herd of young 'uns might be an interesting diversion for an elderly gentleman, he might find the continuing stress too wearing after these sedentary years and be glad to be returned to Buckelwood when we leave.

The debt to cats is herewith partially discharged with this, my fiftieth published book.

Everglades Rod and Gun Club
Everglades, Florida
May 19, 1964

Also by John D. MacDonald

THE EMPTY TRAP   T2870   75¢

Lloyd Wescott was a big boy who knew big money didn't smell like roses. When he was hired to build and run the Green Oasis, he didn't have to ask the pedigree of its owner or where the backing came from. He didn't care. As long as the place was legit and he could run it clean as a whistle.

But just you try to whistle when the Big Man moves in, when skimming is the least of what's going on in the casino, when the quiet luxury is crawling with contract guns, and when a soft, beautiful woman looks at you with love and fear and the desperate longing to escape. That's how it started for Lloyd Wescott—and it ended in passion, murder, and outraged vengeance.

DEADLY WELCOME   M2872   95¢

Alex Doyle left Ramona Beach, Florida, when he was 18, never expecting to get involved with that lousy town or its small-minded people again. But the Defense Department wouldn't let him off the hook, and Doyle found himself submerged once again in the perplexing circumstances which made him split in the first place: venomous gossip, a psychotic police officer, the melancholy recollection of past encounters with the local sex kitten.

|FAWCETT|

Wherever Paperbacks Are Sold

If your bookdealer is sold out, send cover price plus 15¢ each for postage and handling to Mail Order Department, Fawcett Publications, Inc., Greenwich, Connecticut 06830. Please order by number and title. Catalog available on request.